MW00964810

Top 129 Content Marketing Tools

Byron White

Chair, Content Marketing Conference
CEO, WriterAccess

International Standard Book Number: 978-1-60275-059-3

This book is intended for use as an informational guide and entertainment purposes and should not be used as a substitute for any professional medical care or treatment, professional legal advice or professional financial guidance.

CONTENTS

Introduction

Where's all this content going to come from?

If this is the question you've been asking yourself, you've come to the right place.

It's a new era of marketing. Creating value through informational content that is relevant, interesting and useful is the driver for success. Arming yourself with the right tools is critical.

Forward-thinking companies are joining the content marketing revolution -- gathering ideas, developing stories, and publishing a steady stream of content to engage readers and keep them coming back for more.

But planning, creating, optimizing, and distributing all this amazing content is challenging. Not to mention analyzing performance and managing the process in an efficient, effective way.

To help you join the content marketing revolution, we tracked down the top 130 content marketing tools available. Each tool is hand-picked and vetted for performance. We scoured the social sphere for user feedback and bundled it in a book that we hope will guide and enlighten you.

We also included bios of the top content marketing practitioners speaking at the 2016 Content Marketing Conference, an annual gathering of companies, writers, industry experts and thought leaders.

Byron White, founder and chair of Content Marketing Conference, is a content marketing revolutionary, serial entrepreneur, published author, popular speaker, and great storyteller.

Now get out there, fire up some tools, and start creating the amazing content that will help your company thrive.

Opening Remarks

Welcome Content Marketing Conference Attendees!

With four billion content assets published daily, it's getting more and more challenging to make content marketing work these days. Customers are bombarded with information they don't want or need, and it's up to us to help cut the clutter and find a better way.

Over the next few days, we're going to hit the reset button when it comes to content marketing. We'll learn what's new and what's next. Out with the old and what's not working. In with new methodology and technology that's required for success.

Once again, your wants and needs are the centerpiece of the conference. We know you want time-saving hacks and exceptional advice that you can put to work, fast. Peer-to-peer learning is also tops on your list. But what you really want and need is great advice from proven professionals, that inspire you to WOW your readers, customers and fans.

To make this all happen, we spent months hand selected 30 speakers and four keynotes, defining the topics that will engage, enlighten and entertain.

Carmine Gallo was a big help with our mission this year. His book *Talk Like TED* offers nine elements for powerful presentations learned from 500 TED Talks.

1. Passion leads to mastery
2. Stories illustrate, illuminate and inspire
3. Relentless practice is required for emotional connection
4. Reveal something new or package it differently
5. Feature at least one jaw dropping moment
6. Humor lowers defenses and makes you way more likable
7. Keep the attention, 18 minutes is ideal, (or break every 10)
8. Paint the picture with multisensory components
9. Be authentic, open and transparent (Don't be phony)

As it turns out, these nine presentation elements apply to content marketing in general. Content marketing is more about the "content" and delivery, and less about the marketing.

All our speakers received a copy of Carmine's book months ago. Several have performed TED Talks, and many are published authors. You'll hear the passion they have for their topics, and important elements, with delivery that makes you want to learn what's next.

Thanks you all for this opportunity to perform, entertain, and advance your career and knowledge base at CMC 2016.

Write On!
Byron White

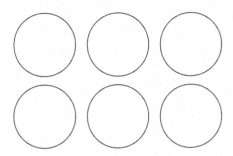

Content Planning

Tools for planning, organization, collaboration, scheduling, surveys, wireframing, and calendaring

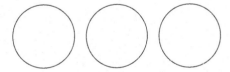

Basecamp

basecamp.com
Powerful collaboration and task management platform

Introduced in 2004, Basecamp has come a long way during the past dozen years to become a well-respected and widely used project management and collaboration tool. During the past decade, new tools and features have been rolled out, tested, weighed and discarded as needed to produce a streamlined set of very useful tools that take a project from its inception all the way to the end product.

Functions are grouped according to their use within the project management process, providing plenty of options for remote collaboration and delegation. In addition to assigning and managing tasks, Basecamp 3, the current version, includes messaging and live chat, and users can upload and share documents and files along the way.

Pros

Basecamp 3 includes a comprehensive array of functions, some of which were carried over from earlier versions and some of which are completely new or substantially retooled. It all begins with task management functions that allow users to assign and track each step of a project, supported by its message board, which is designed to look and feel a lot like Facebook for ease of use. The Campfires tool lets you chat with team members in real-time, Pings provide instant private message capability and automatic check-ins keep everyone on task. Need a quick overview of what everyone's doing? The platform offers an easy-to-scan "bird's eye view" of your group's latest activity.

Cons

Any time new software is released, there are always some kinks to be worked out, and Basecamp 3 comes with a bit of a learning curve, even for those who may have had experience with an earlier version. Some features may be a bit sluggish, and the reporting capabilities are not as robust as some businesses may want. Also, if you're looking for the free version, it's no longer available (unless you're a teacher).

CoSchedule

coschedule.com

Content planning with WordPress integration

CoSchedule is an editorial planning and management tool that integrates directly with WordPress, enabling you and your team to collaborate on and develop an editorial calendar, planning, publishing and promoting content right from the dashboard. Tasks can be assigned to individual team members and the collaboration tools allow comments and feedback during the content and calendar development processes, plus the calendars you create can serve as a basis for "reminders" of subject matter that should be revisited on a routine basis. CoSchedule also facilitates curation of other relevant content to promote greater engagement and visibility and grow your authority as a thought-leader.

Pros

CoSchedule's drag-and-drop function can be used in the calendar view to reschedule posts and automatically update all its associated social media without the need to update each date field individually. Unlike some similar systems that only allow finished posts to be placed on the calendar, CoSchedule also allows drafts to be tentatively scheduled so you can see your complete calendar even while content is still in the creation stages. CoSchedule also makes it easy to share image posts, a feature lacking in some competitors. Plus, Google Analytics tags can be added automatically to your links for better tracking capability, and bit.ly integration lets you keep close tabs on social shares.

Cons

The biggest drawback to CoSchedule is that you need to have a self-hosted WordPress blog in order to take advantage of its most convenient features, but that doesn't mean you have to compose in WordPress. CoSchedule integrates with plenty of other platforms, including Google Docs and Evernote, and you also have the option to export to an HTML file if you prefer to publish using another platform like Blogger, SquareSpace or even WordPress.com.

DivvyHQ

divvyhq.com

Whip project teams into tip-top shape

DivvyHQ is a cloud-based project management tool with specific functionality for content managers and teams. Calendars, workflow tools and social publishing functions let you divvy up content planning, creation and publishing work without losing control over the process. Unlike a number of other platforms, DivvyHQ doesn't concentrate solely on digital content such as blog posts and social media posts; teams can incorporate other marketing plans into the framework and work together to create e-books, videos, print publications, press releases and other content.

Default workflows provide out-of-the-box management for entire content teams, including copywriters, designers, editors and publishers. Content managers can also plan unique projects via the tool's task management functions, which offer progress tracking, work logging and template creation. Since many content managers drive more than one project at a time — often for more than one client — DivvyHQ provides unlimited calendar creation. You can share each calendar with the individuals you choose, letting you silo work as needed.

Pros

As a content planning tool, DivvyHQ is a master for managing teams. A user-friendly dashboard makes quick updates simple and keeps everyone on track while unlimited calendar management aligns well with multiproject and team approaches. Workflow management reduces risk of lost tasks or forgotten content and gives you the ability to plan content for multimedia or offline needs. The platform allows for content creation and social publishing all in one place and even has a parking lot for unused ideas. Your content is also highly protected on secure cloud servers, with backups every three hours.

Cons

While DivvyHQ may be a fantastic choice for agencies and larger organizations fielding multiple teams, it's not the way to go for a single freelancer or the owner of one site. Even the least expensive of the three packages, the Lite package, could still be cost-prohibitive for smaller businesses on tighter budgets. The Lite package is also missing the handy social publishing function. Only the highest-cost package, Enterprise, comes with any level of support.

GatherContent
gathercontent.com
Cleans up the content creation process

Even a single piece of online content can have numerous components, including text, graphics, photos, tables and charts. Now, multiply that single piece of content by the dozens of pieces your business creates on a regular basis, and you can end up with one big mess. The mess comes from forgetting who is working on what or when you told people their tasks were due. More mess comes from glitchy formats and missed deadlines, especially when you're not sure who to track down for delivery.

Clean up the mess with GatherContent. This online platform allows you to plan, organize and collaborate on all types of Web content for seamless, on-time results. Tools let you collate content, keep tabs on creators to eliminate delays, prep content for approval, and fully customize your content workflow.

Pros
The ability to easily organize and track all the pieces of a content puzzle is golden, as is the ability to keep solid track of which producers are working up to par and those who are consistently late with their content deliveries. Sharing capabilities let you send content to project managers, editors or anyone else who needs to review or approve it. The platform also gives you a central location where you can store all your finished content, making it easy for Web designers to access and retrieve material as needed.

Cons
The platform will let you store and access content, but it doesn't provide any tools for optimizing it. You won't find a spell checker, search engine optimization keyword options, or quick publishing to your favorite platform through application programming interface

integrations. That means there's no easy posting of your content on WordPress or other content management systems. Each page that needs an update or change must be changed individually, which can end up being a massive time-eater if you have multiple pages that need altering. Although you can customize the workflow to meet your needs, you can't fine-tune any of the features.

Hootsuite
hootsuite.com
Social engagement geared for SEM

Hootsuite is a social media management system, or SMMS, that helps businesses manage all their social media accounts in one place. It offers an expansive set of tools (that vary based on the subscription level) to monitor and directly respond to customer feedback and post updates across multiple social media accounts without the need to log in to each account separately. Plus, Hootsuite provides in-depth analytics to help you identify your most effective campaigns, along with a tool to help businesses find and curate shareable content, one of the most cumbersome tasks of any SMMS team.

Pros
Hootsuite remains a top SMMS, and it regularly updates its features to make the platform more user-friendly and robust. The platform features a comprehensive array of analytics options, with a couple of notable exceptions listed below. If you use a team to manage to manage your social media, Hootsuite makes it easy to assign action tasks to different team members, which is especially useful for businesses that receive a lot of customer feedback. Plus, it features cross-compatibility with all modern browsers, including mobile versions, and you can use any version of Hootsuite – even the free one – to manage Google+, a feature formerly available only in the costly Enterprise plan.

Cons
Hootsuite provides its own URL shorteners which it requires you to use, and if you add links using other shorteners like bit.ly or SumAll, the traffic from those links won't be included in your Hootsuite report.

You can upgrade to a vanity URL, but the price is steep – about $50 per month as of this writing. Pricing can be steep for larger companies interested in the Enterprise option, available for businesses with more than 10 users. If your business uses the bulk scheduling option or an RSS feed, Hootsuite only posts the text without images, which can decrease the number of click-throughs you get.

Jumpchart

jumpchart.com
Jumpstart your website design

Planning and designing a website can be far less painful with the online wireframing service of Jumpchart. Instead of relying on scribbled sketches on pads of paper, you can take your website creation online with tools that help you plan a site's architecture, organize its navigation, design its aesthetics and create its content. Information architects, designers, copywriters, project managers and all other team members can collaborate on the site at the same time, with all changes, approvals and input automatically tracked. Team members can also view each other's work, sharing comments and feedback. The subscription-based service offers its smallest package for free, with the largest package weighing in at $50 per month or $400 per year.

Pros
From the initial design of the site's structure to the composition of content, all the tools needed to plan a website are in a single space. Using Jumpchart far outweighs working with multiple applications to get the full job done. The free package is a plus, and several different Jumpchart packages offer varying amounts of projects and storage to meet the needs of different users. Larger packages come equipped with bonus features, such as versioning and export services. Newbies without much website planning experience will appreciate the clean and intuitive interface that makes the process easy.

Cons
The free package has a nice price, but it seems to serve as more of a teaser than anything else. It only supports a single, 10-page project

with a maximum of two users. All the really good stuff comes with a price. The Jumpchart software is geared toward site layouts with basic or limited complexity and is unable to accommodate precise adjustments or complicated navigation structures. You'll also be limited to using Jumpchart as an organizational tool, as it offers no tools for creating your site's actual interface. The larger packages do, however, let you export your Jumpchart designs to WordPress for the next phase of the website building process.

Kapost

kapost.com
Soup-to-nuts content platform

Turning a good idea into great piece of content can be tough enough, and that's even before you get to the distribution part of the deal. Kapost was invented to tackle the task with a complete soup-to-nuts platform that guides you through every step of the process. Before you even put fingers to keyboard, you can plan out the entire lifespan of your content, so you know exactly who you're writing for and where that content is going.

Tools let you map your buyer personas, plan and organize your content on a built-in calendar, customize your various content types and campaigns, and designate where your content will eventually land for the biggest impact. Kapost also knows collaboration is key, so it provides a series of tools designed to keep different employees and departments connected on the projects specifically assigned to them.

Pros

High marks go to the Kapost content auditor, a tool that gathers the different types of content you've already published. This can include everything from YouTube videos to business blogs to articles or reports on your website. You can then organize and categorize the existing content based on the stage of the buying process it targets, the buyer persona it's been assigned to, and various other factors. The end result is a detailed overview of all your content on a user-friendly dashboard, which allows you to keep track of the status and effectiveness of all your in-progress campaigns.

Cons

As comprehensive as Kapost may be, it still has a few limitations that prevent it from being a stand-alone solution. Sure, you'll get detailed analytics that shed insight into how your published content is being perceived, but you won't be treated to any sales-performance-related analytics. You won't be able to tell how many leads a particular piece has generated over time, for example, which can be an essential statistic when it comes to future planning and production. Another downside is the lack of integration abilities, with no straightforward way to integrate your existing email marketing or other automation systems into the Kapost platform.

Opal

workwithopal.com
Recipe for content-planning success

You know that saying about too many cooks spoiling the soup? The same thing can happen with content planning if people are chopping, dicing and mixing in ideas with no real organization in place. Opal gives you that organization in the form of a collaborative content planning app that lets you plan all of your content, promotions and campaigns in a single location. Multiple users can work on content planning using Opal, whether they are in the same office or halfway around the world. The main aims of this subscription-based app are to increase efficiency, boost productivity, support collaboration and promote consistent brand messaging across all channels. It would be tough to find any chef who didn't appreciate that.

Pros

Real-time discussions help all the cooks stay in line, with on-the-spot content change-tracking, feedback and discussion. You no longer have to play email ping-pong but can instead converse with team members using a chat interface within the document itself. This saves time, reduces misunderstandings and encourages collaboration. The ability to see all your in-progress content in a single place is another plus, as is the calendar feature, which you can use as a visual planning tool. A top chef still gets the final say-so, with an approval option that won't release content until the assigned approvers give the OK. Nestle, NASA, Levi's and Target are just a few of the well-known brands that swear by Opal.

Cons

Opal doesn't publish a pricing structure on its website, typically a sign that the service is going to be costly. Anyone interested must request a quote or a demo, which potentially sets the stage for a flurry of sales pitches. Smaller brands and startups may not want to even bother requesting a quote, not only because of the significant investment but also because many of Opal's distinguishing features, such as cloud-based collaboration, are geared toward larger brands with users in multiple locations.

Ripenn

ripenn.com
Fueling your audience with content it wants

You could have the best content distribution and marketing strategies in the world, but they'll amount to nothing if you ultimately fail to meet the needs of your target audience with the content itself. Ripenn can help you meet those needs and then some. This streamlined platform not only enables you to collect new ideas for content, but it gives you the means to efficiently execute their ultimate creation and distribution for the greatest impact. Content planning is handled from one straightforward, easy-to-use interface similar to a traditional desktop calendar. You can keep track of content ideas, the content creation progress and even publishing dates all from the same screen — making it easy to visualize where your content is coming from and where it will eventually go.

Pros

The major strength of Ripenn comes from the way it enables easy collaboration, even among people who work in different departments or locations within the same organization. Everyone can contribute to Ripenn directly from their Web browser of choice after installing one basic extension. If anyone, anywhere has a killer idea for a piece of content, the idea is immediately available to everyone else, so it can be acted on quickly and efficiently. Another plus is Ripenn's dedicated mobile app, which gives you access to publishing plans and work in progress from any mobile device.

The collaboration features also extends to content creation itself, as the document editor allows teams of people to write together from different endpoints. All versions of a document can be easily managed within the same user interface. This lets you compare changes, see which user contributed specific elements, and otherwise ensure all pieces of the content puzzle are coming together to create a single, highly effective whole.

Cons

It's tough to find anyone saying anything negative about Ripenn, but that's mainly because it's tough to find any reviews at all. All that collaboration comes with a price, of course, but the cost is not astronomical. The basic plan of $19 per month allows for one editor and five contributors, but it also leaves out all the juicy content suggestions that can give you the heftiest edge. Plan prices go up to $49 per month for 10 editors, unlimited contributors and, yes, those juicy content suggestions.

ScribbleLive

scribblelive.com
Real-time content with real-time analytics

What started as a live blogging platform in 2008 has since blossomed into a full-blown content engagement platform that aims to boost your content marketing efforts. Its distinguishing feature is a focus on real-time content creation and publication, complete with real-time, automatic updates that don't require viewers to refresh the page.

The platform is ideal for sports, breaking news, Q&A sessions and ongoing events that deserve immediate updates. Business-to-business content marketers can use ScribbleLive to provide up-to-the-minute coverage from conventions, conferences and other live events. The company's growth has come from a number of funding rounds, and it got big enough by June 2014 to acquire its competitor, CoveritLive. Both platforms will continue to develop independently.

Pros

ScribbleLive's biggest claim to fame is its ability to provide all types of live, real-time content — along with real-time analytics. Content can include tweets, text messages, voice mails, emails, photos, social media updates and video. All content can additionally be posted and edited right from the browser-based platform without the need for special software.

The ease and scope of use are another plus. Mobile apps for Android and iOS let you produce content anytime, anywhere, and multiple users in a single organization can work on live blogs simultaneously. One more plus is the ability to enrich your visitors' experience through content creation, with relevant Twitter hashtags and posts from involved users pulled into your content as you're creating it.

Cons

Although content curation from blogs and Twitter is spot-on, curation from Facebook is limited due to Facebook's privacy settings. Any event or post that relies heavily on Facebook content will thus be at a major disadvantage. Another con only applies if you're the type who tends to get carried away with too much of a good thing. The ease of posting can lead to oversaturation, which can end up repelling your audience. Instead of posting every single thing that is done or said at an event, users can create an outline in advance and focus on the most exciting photos, videos and quotes.

Sprout

sproutsocial.com
Context-based engagement for happier customers

Sprout is a content engagement tool that focuses on a "contextual" approach to customer relations. What does that mean? If you've ever been on the receiving end of a disjointed CSR engagement that makes you feel like you're continually repeating your initial issue, you already have a good idea.

When a Sprout user replies to feedback, the entire conversation "pops" up, including the customer's contact info, so the responses are made within the context of the entire conversation, not isolated comments or questions. Contextual engagement fosters a team approach while still supporting a cohesive experience for the customer. Plus, like other content engagement systems, Sprout offers the ability to publish across multiple platforms using a comprehensive set of publishing tools via a well-organized dashboard.

Pros

Sprout offers a Smart Inbox to manage all social activity is a single stream, making it easier to track and respond. Robust publishing tools make it easy to share a variety of content across multiple social platforms, and Sprout's scheduling functionality supports auto-publishing for greater ease. Responses can be made from within the dashboard and feature a complete comment history, so there's no need to search for previous comments to keep responses in context. Twitter keyword functionality and robust discovery tools help your business determine which accounts to follow for the greatest visibility and engagement. Plus, Sprout offers you the option to export to PDF or Excel files, and it also offers workflow management options to assign and manage specific tasks.

Cons

Like Hootsuite, pricing is made on a per-participant basis, so if you have a large team managing your content, Sprout can get pretty pricey. While it does provide compatibility with Facebook, Twitter, Google+ and LinkedIn. Sprout does not (yet) interface with Pinterest or Instagram, so if your company depends on those platforms for a significant share of its feedback or promotion, Sprout may not be the best option. However, the Sprout team does make frequent updates, so it's worth checking to see if they've expanded to include these two platforms.

SurveyGizmo
surveygizmo.com
Understand your audience better with simple surveys

SurveyGizmo is a survey-creation tool that offers a comprehensive array of advanced features to make survey creation simple and straightforward. The platform supports all types of survey formats, including text and multiple choice, and surveys can be distributed via email or social media using the user-friendly interface. Advanced, one-click reporting and real-time updates and notifications let you create highly interactive surveys that automatically evolve based on each respondent's answers to add or eliminate questions or perform other actions for a truly custom experience.

Pros

SurveyGizmo allows pretty much complete customization of surveys, including the colors, sizes, layout and images, to integrate seamlessly with your brand experience. Distribution across multiple platforms is simple and can be performed via the dashboard without leaving the program. Real-time interaction keeps your audience engaged while gathering hyper-targeted information that can help you build a more responsive campaign. Plus, SurveyGizmo also integrates well with leading tools like Salesforce and Zapier. Direct phone support helps you get the most from your subscription and can make learning the platform and customizing it even easier.

Cons

While SurveyGizmo provides a comprehensive array of features, all those bells and whistles come at a price, and the average cost tends to be higher than similar survey software that may not offer quite as many features. Surveys are not an ideal type of content for every business, product or service, so be sure it suits your needs before making the leap.

Trello

trello.com
Virtual whiteboard for intuitive project management

Trello is a project management tool that's designed for virtual collaboration, making it easy to manage your team wherever the members may be. Think of a giant whiteboard where you and your team members can post and share ideas and images, keep track of to-do lists, brainstorm on content ideas and projects, create checklists and perform myriad other project management tasks, and you'll have a pretty good idea of what Trello is and does. Trello enables sharing lists or individual task cards with an entire team, a subset of members or a single member, and files can be added from your own hard drive or right from the cloud via services such as Box, Dropbox, Google Drive and OneDrive.

Pros

Trello is very simple to use, with an intuitive interface that's simple to set up and manage, featuring a drag-and-drop interface and tags or "stickers" for greater organization. The basic version is also free to use, so for businesses with limited budgets or companies and agencies that don't have a lot of experience using virtual project management solutions, Trello can be a great way to get your feet wet. Sharing links and inviting collaboration, even from non-team members, is fairly straightforward, and you can print your boards directly to PDFs for record-keeping.

Cons

One of the reasons Trello is easy to use is because its scope and functionality are fairly basic, thanks to a relatively limited number of tools and features. While this can be a "pro" for businesses with basic project management needs, other companies with larger and more complicated projects may find it too limiting. A few truly useful features, like file exports, are only available in paid versions.

TweetDeck

tweetdeck.twitter.com
Manage multiple Twitter feeds in real-time

TweetDeck is a dedicated tool for Twitter that allows you to post tweets and track replies, hashtags and conversations over one or more Twitter accounts and in real time, for better and more responsive engagement. Tools enable users to schedule future tweets, and a handy notification feature sends out alerts when one of the tweets you post receives a reply.

The platform is designed to provide a side-by-side, real-time view of tweets and conversations, which can be especially useful for businesses that depend on Twitter for customer engagement, feedback and response, as well as for those who need to monitor multiple Twitter feeds throughout the day. TweetDeck is completely free no matter how many accounts are connected, and both browser and downloadable apps are available.

Pros

TweetDeck is free, which makes it a good, basic tool for businesses and agencies of all sizes. The ability to schedule tweets in advance makes content management much simpler, especially when Twitter forms the core of your marketing and social media campaigns. Desktop notifications help ensure you never miss an opportunity to reply or engage so customers enjoy a more personal experience with your brand.

Cons

TweetDeck only works with Twitter, which means if you use other social media platforms on a regular basis for your marketing campaigns, you'll need to search for another tool to handle them. And those notifications that are so handy to have? They're only available on the software version. TweetDeck doesn't offer any statistics, analytics or reporting, and there is no ability to assign or manage tasks, which can prove problematic when multiple team members are responding to tweets throughout the day.

UXPin

Uxpin.com
Theme-based design on demand

Having a great website begins with the basics, and UXPin provides an excellent resource for content planning through wireframing. Users can design device-specific formats, which include Android, iPhone, Web and browser-specific functionality. As a design platform, UXPin offers a place to combine all of a business's existing designs from Sketch, Photoshop, or freehand drawing on tablets without sacrificing the ability to work within existing layers. UXPin takes the initial planning phase further by offering prototyping, presentation creation, usability tests and mock-up creation.

Pros

A subscription to UXPin starts with a free trial – everyone loves a freebie. The site also offers a host of e-books, examples for inspiration, and a guided tour for novice designers. UXPin maintains a strict security policy, which serves a dual function of increasing accountability and keeping your content secure.

Once your wireframe is completed, upload your content directly in UXPin, and share an accessible mock-up with your team members, business partners or even potential customers. You can select your subscription to meet your needs, which range from basic to enterprise applications. Users can create an infinite number of projects, making the creation and optimization process simpler and faster.

Cons

Although it is among the most inexpensive content tools available, UXPin does have some drawbacks. The free trial only lasts seven days. However, it may be extended up to 30 days, in five- to 10-day increments, if you share your experience on Twitter, Facebook or Google Plus. The biggest perk of UXPin – the ability to allow others to comment on your creation in a live environment – is also UXPin's greatest drawback. The system's preview mode allows your design to function as if it's already been published. Unfortunately, UXPin lacks a notification system, resulting in the need to regularly check for new comments.

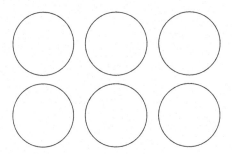

Content Creation

Tools for finding writers, quiz making, graphic creation, infographic creation, webinar creation, podcast creation, and event creation

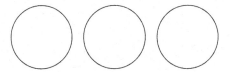

99Designs

99designs.com
Custom-designed content in contest form

99Designs is comparable to crowdfunding for virtually any of type of design, which includes graphic design, website design, promotional materials, brochures, social media mock-ups, 3D illustrations, book layouts, and more. With more than 1,128,000 designers, 99Designs has one of the largest pools of talent on the globe.

The site operates as a contest. You can request designs from freelancers around the globe, and after seven days, select a winner. When you include as many details in your contest as possible, submitted designs will be of better quality and align with your expectations. Price ranges from $200 to $1,000 and is determined as you see fit, which may include a healthy tip to intrigue to the best designers.

Pros

Accessing a pool of talented designers, 99Designs offers the cheapest way to get the most ideas at the lowest price. Templated order designs make it easy to launch your contest, but 99Designs offers human support to ensure your contest launches as soon as possible. Select among four design packages. The review process is similar to other content creation sites. Request revisions, provide feedback to designers, and rate a designer's work. If you find a designer that you love, you can work with them exclusively on future projects as well.

Cons

You don't get to keep and use all submitted designs. You only retain the copyright to the submission of the winner. All rights to other designs revert back to the "losers" of the contest. If you cannot explain your needs fully, submitted designs will be of poor quality. Since the design package-based system grants access to different levels of skill among freelance designers, paying for the lowest tier means your design may not be amazing. The weeklong deadline to select a winner is also a drawback, especially when the site does not discuss any form of refund if you're dissatisfied.

Adobe Creative Cloud

adobe.com/creativecloud.html
Prime combination of Adobe's creativity tools

Adobe is one of the best-known technologies for creating graphics, stories, and nearly any other form of content. Adobe Creative Cloud uses cloud-based technologies to grant you access to the most comprehensive collection of Adobe creation products. This includes Photoshop, Illustrator, InDesign and Adobe Premiere Pro. The Creative Cloud further ensures all members of your team are on the same page and enables collaborative efforts to produce, manage and distribute created materials

Pros

Adobe Creative Cloud includes access to the Creative Cloud libraries, such as Adobe Stock. You may access the Creative Cloud from desktop and mobile devices, allowing for content creation while traveling. Compared to the cost of purchasing individual licenses for each terminal and user, the Adobe Creative Cloud is extremely cost-effective. You can also purchase individual products, and the cost of packages range from $9.99 to $79.98.

If you plan on using Adobe Creative Cloud for business purposes, you can purchase a set number of licenses for use in your team at a discounted rate, and you receive dedicated, around-the-clock technical support. The amount of storage space within the Creative Cloud is also expanded to 100 gigabytes.

Cons

If you underestimate your needs, you could end up spending much more on Adobe Creative Cloud than you intend to. For example, you could decide to purchase several photography apps individually rather than the full package of Adobe services. If rapid growth of your business means you need to purchase other services that are part of the Adobe Creative Cloud within a few months, you may end up spending more for each item individually than you would have for the full package at the beginning. If you only want to use Adobe Creative Cloud on a month-to-month basis, 12 months paid for individually costs more than selecting an annual plan.

Audacity

Audacityteam.org
Audio does the talking

Audacity is your one-stop shopping tool for audio streaming, capture and editing. Nearly any type of recording can be made in Audacity, and users have the capability to edit audio tracks in striking detail. Most importantly, Audacity is completely free.

Pros

Most operating systems support the use of Audacity, and recent fixes have made Audacity compatible with Linux systems. Users can manage multiple recordings, monitor volume levels, record from a microphone, USB or line-input, and playback audio on computers that are running Windows Vista or newer systems.
Other benefits of Audacity include the ability to set recordings on timers, sound-activated recording, dub over tracks, record low-latency sounds and record on multiple channels.

Cons

Logic dictates Audacity should run on any device, but the proprietary software in Audacity is incompatible with the storage capabilities of most mobile devices and tablet computers. Audacity cannot run as a standalone software on Chromebooks, and users must ensure plenty of space is available to run Audacity in a desktop environment.

Unfortunately, the popularity of Audacity has led to trickery among advertisers, and some advertisers charge a subscription fee to access a copy of the Audacity download file, which should be free. Audacity is incapable of refunding money spent when Audacity is downloaded through third-party entities. Ultimately, vigilance is the most important part of understanding how to use and access Audacity as the developers intended.

Boost Media

boostmedia.com
Win the PPC war with targeted campaigns

Boost Media is a creative optimization platform, providing powerful tools and critical insight to help businesses and content managers create, test and then optimize their ads across multiple platforms for finely tuned and highly targeted campaigns. Developed to provide a superior alternative to the one-size-fits-all approach to template-driven ad campaigns, the Boost Media platform brings together creatives like writers and designers to create targeted, scaled campaigns that can be tested side-by-side so you can see – literally – which approach is most effective for your target audience.

Pros

Boost Media uses actual creatives to develop and optimize ad campaigns for a richer and more personalized experience for customers, sourcing professional writers and designers and connecting via the cloud to collaborate on campaigns that feel more relevant than those derived from templates. Its contest format lets you "try before you buy," testing campaigns against each other so you can make the most of your advertising budget. The interface is simple to use, enabling you to establish your own guidelines and parameters for each ad campaign. Once submissions are received, you have the option of approving them yourself or having a dedicated Customer Success Manager handle that task for you. Once an ad is approved, it goes live automatically, and you only pay for the ads that wind up "winning."

Cons

There's no doubt optimizing an ad campaign can have a big payout, but despite its simple interface, Boost Media can be time-consuming to use, requiring you to post an initial ad against which challenger ads are tested. For companies or agencies with smaller staffs, dedicating the resources needed to manage each ad campaign until a winner is identified may be too costly.

Canva

canva.com
Crop, resize and edit on your terms

Photos and images are critical to a successful marketing campaign, and Canva is one of the best resources for editing images. Canva allows you to retake control over how your photos appear without the limitations of Microsoft Paint. Import your designs directly into Canva in various layers to make the design process easier. Furthermore, the site allows you to create an account quickly by signing in with Facebook or your Google account.

Pros

Unlike the majority of content creation tools, Canva is completely free. You do not have to sign up for lengthy downloads or guides, but the developers include plenty of resources to learn more about the tool's functionality. A 23-second tutorial is available to show new users how to navigate the system. Add headings, subtitles, charts, graphs, grids and more without the confusion of more advanced editors.

Upon completing an image in Canva, download the image in PDF for print or PDF for Web. Other download options include JPG and PNG formats as well. If you want to share the image, you can set the image to public, and others may edit it accordingly.

Cons

It is difficult to find problems with Canva, but that does not mean none exist. If you log out without downloading or saving the image, you will lose it. Furthermore, sharing an image (making it public) does not include a URL. Sharing the image requires the email address of the recipient. As a result, this editing tool is not the best for use among team projects.

Contently

contently.com
High-end content festival

If you don't have quality content in today's marketing arena, you don't have squat. Contently can help you fix that, stocking your company with the high-end content you need to compete in the digital marketing landscape. The subscription-based platform combines three key components to do it. The first is access to a large pool of talented freelancers along with hard-hitting content strategies. The second is powerful software that lets you oversee content creation, approval, distribution and performance. The third is input from Contently's own service team, which has been helping to improve all types of content since the company's inception in 2010.

Pros

Contently's freelance network includes but doesn't stop at a large cache of freelance writers. The talent pool spans some 60 countries and is stocked with more than 45,000 journalists, graphic designers, photographers and producers. The high pay attracts premium talent, and Contently performs stringent reviews before anyone is invited to join the network. Even if you don't want help from the freelancers available through the platform, you can still subscribe and use the software to manage your in-house team of content creation talent. Sophisticated analytics are part of the software-as-a-service package, which also includes a calendar, workflow tracking and management of all your content assets in a single location.

Cons

Contently is an enterprise solution, with enterprise prices, and layered pricing based on platform fees, service fees and writer fees, all separate yet bundled. The least expensive package starts at $3,000 per month and increases from there to over $25,000. It's a solution designed for big companies with big budgets.

GoAnimate

goanimate.com
DIY video and animation builder

Animation transforms surfing and browsing the Internet into an interactive process. GoAnimate enables users to customize animations with simple tools, styles and features. The animations are created by dragging and dropping different, predesigned characters, images and functions into the animation. The process is made simple, through the use of five steps, including scripting and storyboarding, voice recording, actual animating, audio insertion and publishing. Using GoAnimate, animations can be made in less than five minutes.

Pros

If you want to create an animation in as little time as possible, GoAnimate is your solution. The site offers a free trial for 14 days of the premium subscription, which normally costs $79 per month. Additionally, all subscriptions include at least one design seat in the tool, video downloads of at least 720p quality, unlimited video production, direct export to external sites, and the ability to import external files into the animation. GoAnimate also places an emphasis on security and privacy among all subscriptions, and users can select between 40 and 100 audio tracks, depending on the type of subscription selected, to use in the animation.

Cons

Because of the limitations of drag-and-drop animation, GoAnimate offers little hope for highly skilled, high quality, professional videos. Additionally, the least expensive subscription costs $39 per month, and its features are minimal when compared to higher tiers. The GoAnimate logo is present on the basic subscription, and you cannot import your own fonts unless you upgrade to a premium tier of service. Even the largest, more beneficial subscription, which costs $159 per month, does not achieve the high-quality animations that many users demand.

Piktochart

piktochart.com
Infographic generation made simple

If you want to generate traffic to your website, simply presenting information in plain text form is not enough. Piktochart makes creating visually appealing infographics easy. Start with a design and template. You can edit text, fonts or colors and add photos, videos, interactive charts and industry-specific illustrations or icons to your design.

Offering free access to Piktochart for all users, developers of the site have managed to gain a loyal following of more than 4 million users. Additionally, Piktochart experts author a blog to help novice designers start their projects. This makes Piktochart an excellent tool for startups, nonprofits and educational institutions.

Pros

The ability to insert texts, graphics, banners, and virtually any other file enables you to edit your infographics or presentations at your convenience directly within Piktochart. The design process can go with you wherever you go. Piktochart is a drag-and-drop tool, which eliminates the need to hire expensive designers. Furthermore, Piktochart allows unlimited creations via free accounts for life. Depending on billing preferences, the Lite subscription costs $15 per month, and the enhanced subscription costs $29 per month

Cons

Choosing a free account limits the number of templates you can access, and your image upload limit is a minimal. Furthermore, free accounts do not include the ability to export documents in PDF format, and a Piktochart logo appears on all graphics in the free and Lite versions. Although you can create infographics and presentations with Piktochart at break-neck speeds, infographics made with the program tend to look similar to many other infographics, which could adversely affect your search engine ranking. Piktochart's customization features are typically more expensive than most other programs.

Prezi

prezi.com
Adaptable, fast presentation creation and management

Prezi is an innovative and useful tool for creating presentations. The strength of a presentation is the key factor in how well an audience receives a presenter at an event or when viewing it on their own terms. As a result, Prezi enables visual storytelling in a conversational manner that can be adapted whenever you need. Templates, custom content, and a number of file types that can be imported means presentation designers have plenty of flexibility to be creative and innovative in their work.

Pros

The basic function behind Prezi enables you to post your presentations without a cost. Your presentations can be made entirely public if you want to enroll as a free account; or you can choose from three different types of subscriptions. If you need to use Prezi for educational purposes, the company offers discounts when signing up with a school email address. Users can access Prezi on any device, and all free account holders have the ability to work offline.

Cons

The benefits of Prezi are also closely related to its drawbacks. If you use the public account for free access, you do not retain any form of copyright over your creations. All material created using the free account can be viewed, searched and reused by the public. Paid subscriptions are only billable in annual format. The minimum cost of using Prezi as a paid subscription is $60 annually, which includes image editing, the ability to work offline and assistance in how to use this resource. Prezi Pro and Prezi Teams offer unlimited storage, but a Prezi Team subscription costs $795 per year for up to five users.

Qzzr

Qzzr.com

Ramp up engagement, build your authority with custom quizzes

Qzzr is an online quiz tool that makes it easy to create interactive quizzes to drive engagement, generate leads, hone marketing objectives and promote your brand. Content marketing data show customers – and especially millennials – expect to be engaged during their customer experience, and not just sold to. Quizzes provide an entertaining and highly-interactive way to engage your audience while also capturing important data about the people who visit your site – and without the use of standard or intrusive questionnaires The Qzzr tool is designed to integrate with leading CRM tools, email marketing tools, and marketing automation systems to facilitate rapid follow-up of prospective leads, and it integrates seamlessly with social platforms like Facebook to boost your likes and shares.

Pros

Qzzr features an easy-to-use interface that makes it very simple to create quizzes of all types and styles, including graded quizzes, outcome quizzes and checklists. Quizzes can be easily customized to suit a specific style or appearance, and images and animated GIFs are supported in addition to text. You can even create quizzes in languages other than English to broaden your reach across borders.

Cons

As a quiz creation platform, Qzzr doesn't have a whole lot of cons, but for quizzes in general, there are a few potential drawbacks. When creating and distributing a quiz, it's imperative to know your audience. While millennials may love quizzes, some audiences may find them annoying or intrusive. Plus, you'll need to do some research to make sure your quizzes are suitable for your audience and their interests, and also to make sure your answers are correct. Posting a quiz with incorrect information or offensive images, or distributing a quiz that's meant to be humorous but winds up hitting a sour note, can wind up backfiring.

Scripted

scripted.com
Expert content, heavy editing

Founded in 2008, San Francisco-based Scripted is an online marketplace that matches up companies and agencies with content writers. Although the name Scripted comes from its original purpose as a screenwriting service, the scope expanded in 2011 to include Web articles, blogs, press releases, social media posts and other types of content. The site boasts expert writers in every subject, from traditional fare to unexpected requests.

Pros

A stringent application process weeds out more than 80 percent of the writers who apply to the marketplace, ensuring that only those who are well-qualified and have expertise in certain areas get through. The site says more than 7,000 freelance writers are ready for action, with client orders offered to only those most qualified to complete them. The platform is hailed as intuitive and easy to understand, with a self-explanatory order form that generally takes about five minutes to complete. True to its roots, Scripted also offers video script writing, a service not found in many content platforms.

Cons

Scripted offers a flat rate, one-size-fits-all approach to pricing, without the ability for customers to pay more to get higher quality content. The editing services are included whether you want them or not, even if you're confident putting the final touches on your own content.

Additional delays can pop up if a writer drops an order, which writers can do with no penalties or repercussions. When this happens, you must launch the order anew, setting the entire process back several days. Clients are also at the mercy of the service when it comes to choosing a specific writer. Clients can set up a list of favorite writers, but cannot select a single writer out of the batch to receive an order, a valuable feature for content creation platforms.

Textbroker

textbroker.com
Custom content

Textbroker has been around for many years, originally based in Germany. Its workforce of writers is global, which opens up all kinds of benefits, and concerns. Inexpensive "text" is the aim of the model, offering very inexpensive prices for content writing. For less complex projects and higher volume work, Textbroker seems to have carved out a niche.

Pros

Unlike some other writing services that charge different fees for different licensing options, you get all rights to the content to use as you wish once an order is completed and accepted. The pricing structure is straightforward and easy to understand, with clients paying fixed rates for the quality desired. Writers are rated on a scale of two to five stars by Textbroker's internal editing team, with five-star writers providing the highest available quality.

You can also add your favorite writers to a personalized list, set up teams, and send orders to individual writers for negotiable rates. Copyscape checks are part of the deal, as is multilingual support if you need it. Textbroker offers support for content in 10 languages, including U.S. English, British English, Spanish, French, German and Dutch. Clients can also request translation assistance from the Textbroker localization team.

Cons

The preset rates have writers earning 5 cents per word at the top of the heap and less than 2 cents per word at the lower ratings. A writer rated at two stars earns a fraction of a penny per word. It may be tough to squeeze quality out of anything less than the highest-rated writers. While clients can set a turnaround time for an order, the timer doesn't start until a writer checks out the order. Orders may sit in the open pool for days before being picked up. Clients must also give writers at least one chance to make revisions before rejecting an article that doesn't meet expectations, leading to additional delays.

Because different authors may pick up a client's orders, the style can vary greatly from piece to piece, producing a disjointed experience for your blog or website. Clients can work around this issue by placing direct orders to their favorite writers, but these often come with a higher price tag.

Visual.ly

visual.ly
Infographics made simple

Infographics are hot, partly because they're highly shareable and partly because most people find visual representation of ideas more engaging and faster to comprehend than a long blog post. The problem is, creating infographics isn't always easy, especially if you aren't a design professional.

Visual.ly was designed to take the headaches out of infographic creation, providing a platform for designers and non-designers alike to come together to create eye-catching graphics. The site provides a selection of templates that can be customized with your own information as well as a community of design pros ready to be matched with more complex design tasks. But infographic creation is just one part of what Visual.ly has to offer. The platform has grown to include other products, like e-books, reports, videos and interactive microsites for full spectrum marketing both on and off your website.

Pros

Free tools and an expanding library of templates lets users jump in and create their own infographics right away. Support and feedback from the site's online community provides troubleshooting and design guidance for better end results. If you don't have a graphic design background, Visual.ly's tools and community help make the infographic creation process less intimidating. Sharing tools help you promote your infographic on the leading social platforms, plus, the site is home to thousands of published infographics to provide plenty of inspiration. If you need professional help creating an infographic, Visual.ly can match you with a design team.

Cons

The number of templates is limited, and for true customization, you'll need to connect with one of the thousands of designers who make up the Visual.ly community.

WriterAccess

writeraccess.com
Go-to writer marketplace

Since its launch in 2010, WriterAccess has exploded as the go-to marketplace for quality content from quality writers, earning a place on the Inc. 5000 list of fastest-growing companies two years in a row. This year the company expanded its talent pool to include translators, editors and content strategists. Unlike many other content-creation platforms, WriterAccess allows clients to communicate with the writers they want to hire through the system, giving businesses more control over the end results and establishing mutually beneficial relationships between clients and writers. Order requests are easy using a ready-made form, and they can include just about anything, blog posts, articles, newsletters, product description, e-books white papers and more.

A pool of more than 14,000 heavily vetted, freelance writers and translators are on board, each one boasting a specific star rating from two to six that indicates their level of proficiency and skill. All writers are US-based. Customers can choose their freelancer by setting up casting calls, launching an order to the crowd, or reviewing the freelancers' comprehensive online profiles to send orders directly to individuals or to a handpicked team. The platform allows customers to select the rates they want to pay based on the quality of writing or translation they need. All work is backed with a 100-percent satisfaction guarantee.

Pros

The ability to pay for the level of quality you want is a major plus, as are three levels of service from which to choose. The Self Service option lets you browse the site and its writers, paying only when you order. Plus Service and Enterprise Service tiers add dedicated account management based on the amount of your up-front deposit, 100 percent of which goes toward writing services. All levels enjoy access to the user-friendly, feature-rich platform equipped to streamline the workflow. Fair, transparent rates and detailed order forms that typically result in few to no rewrites keep thousands of quality writers hanging around for the long term.

Cons
WriterAccess recent expansion of the talent pool in 2016 to Editors, Translator and Content Strategists opens up all kinds of possibilities. Purchasing graphics inside the platform is possible with a partnership with Getty images, but access to designers would be amazing.

Zerys
zerys.com
Writing for a penny

Let's say you still believe that Search Engine Optimization is the driver for content marketing, and you want your content to follow suit. Zerys might be worth considering, with a multi-step platform that puts optimization at the centerpiece of the model in a multi-step approach. The content strategy and planning tools help you discover keywords and topics, compile a list of titles, and set up an editorial calendar. The production platform provides a clean, updated interface and mobile compatibility. The writers come from the platform's immense marketplace, which boasts more than 20,000 writers ready for action. The platform is geared toward marketers and agencies, with a white-label version of the production platform available for the latter.

Pros
Tons of writers and the ability to select a specific writer or a handpicked group mean a wide selection of scribes from which to choose. Low prices are another plus for saving money, with prices for writing starting at 1 cent per word. Another benefit is the ability to set up and check out the platform before you transfer any money into your account. You only have to add money when you're ready to

order content. A money-back guarantee on the writing allows you to get your cash back or try another writer if you're not happy with the material you get from the first one you tried.

Cons

Low prices are a bad omen when it comes to writing quality. True, Zerys does offer rates higher than a single penny, with the order placement system allowing you to pay up to 50 cents per word. In fact, the placement system offers a whole host of options, which can make the ordering process slow and tedious. The platform is not known for its stringent vetting process, with the majority of writing applicants accepted into the fray. Writers are also free to choose their own specialties based on what they feel qualified to write about rather than based on any evidence that proves their qualifications.

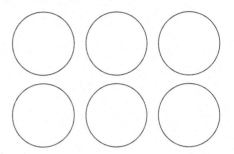

Content Optimization

Tools for SEO, keyword research, A/B testing,
competitive research, influencer insights and
outreach, translation, editing, and grammar

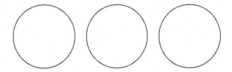

Ahrefs

ahrefs.com
Freshest backlinks on the menu

Mainly used as a sophisticated link-checking tool, Ahrefs boasts the largest and most current indexed database of website backlinks in the world. Ahrefs will also show you all the keywords that any website is ranking for in organic and paid search. This will help you understand what kind of search traffic your competitors get and where your own site stands next to them. The index is updated every 15 minutes, giving you up-to-date information on new and internal links, anchors, linking domains and a domain's top pages. Paid subscriptions give you access to the full suite of Ahrefs tools, which include its backlink reports, organic search reports, keyword ranking reports, website crawl reports and many other extra tools.

Ahrefs "Site Explorer" tool will give you a plethora of data on any website or page that you chose to analyse. You'll be able to see where the backlinks to this website are coming from, what keywords this website is ranking for in search engines and what PPC ads they are running. You'll be able to dig deeper into each of these reports and source the information that you need to outrank your competitors in search. A sampling includes the total number of referring domains, subnets and IP addresses; type of backlinks that point to your site; and a breakdown on the domain extensions, such as .com, .org or .gov. You'll also be privy to link charts outlining link totals as well as new and lost links over a rolling five-month period. And that's just a sampling.

Pros

You can check a competitor's site as easily as you can check your own, giving you valuable insight into what your top competitors are up to. The domain comparison tools let you compare up to five domains, checking out statistics on referring domains as well as link types. The platform can check for both incoming and outgoing links, give you a heads-up on which of your pages generated the most backlinks and social mentions, and provide you with an in-depth bar chart breakdown on anchor text. High speed, ease of use and exportable data options are also on the list of benefits.

Cons

Although Ahrefs is amazing for tracking and reporting on links, it's not as savvy about filling you in on the quality of those links. Sure, the tool does rank sites by importance based upon its own calculations, but it doesn't reveal information on the amount of traffic, traffic quality or authority of the sites. A few high-quality links are much more valuable than a zillion weak ones, and you may need to turn to a more in-depth analytics tool to gauge the quality of links associated with your site.

BrightInfo

brightinfo.com/solution-for-marketers
Intense, data-driven SEO

SEO is everything. It can mean the difference between reaching thousands, if not millions, of new customers and complete failure. BrightInfo is an all-inclusive, do-it-yourself optimization tool. Regardless of your goals and hopes, BrightInfo surpasses many of the capabilities of other optimization tools.

Pros

With BrightInfo, you can take advantage of dynamic content for all optimization packages. BrightInfo includes marketing automation tools and account-based marketing features. If you do not need all of the features included in the minimum package, you can purchase individual optimization tools at varying rates.
BrightInfo also analyzes your prospective consumers' behavior and interests to help you target keywords and content to meet what visitors want. Furthermore, you have the ability to control how and when your pages appear. For example, you could design certain pages to serve as pop ups with a new offer for consumers that were about to leave your site. As a result, you can increase your retargeting efforts and enjoy more conversions through this tool.

Cons

Unlike many SEO tools, BrightInfo is expensive. Pricing for the BrightInfo Platinum is $999 per month, and enterprise applications of BrightInfo are only available through a custom price quote. Content created, distributed or optimized through BrightInfo receive the

BrightInfo branding mark. Enterprise applications of BrightInfo are the only subscription that do not have the BrightInfo branding or logo. Additionally, BrightInfo is limited in the number of allowed subdomains. Silver and gold packages only allow two sub domains per subscriber. Platinum package subscribers may have up to five subdomains, but this is often less than many other SEO tools.

BuzzSumo

Buzzsumo.com
Powerful content booster

Reaching the right audience with your content is one of your biggest dreams. And those dreams can align more closely with reality with help from BuzzSumo. This content marketing management platform simplifies the often complicated task of ensuring that your content is getting the attention it deserves. It does this through a host of beneficial features that include discovering the hottest content, alerting you to content containing your chosen keywords or specifications, reaching out to influencers, researching your competitors, researching and planning your own content and, of course, analyzing its performance. Put everything together and you have one powerful tool for ensuring that your content is indeed reaching the right audience, perhaps even more accurately than you dreamed.

Pros

Tons of pros come packed in BuzzSumo, with every featuring offering multiple ways to ensure that you're creating the unique, high-quality content that your targeted audience wants to read. One example is a quick topic search, which lets you see the most recent posts on that topic that are doing well online. This insight allows you to add your own take on the topic, ensuring that it's different from the rest yet posted in the same channels where the topic is really taking off. BuzzSumo also lets you filter content according to its format, such as videos, giveaways, articles and others, allowing you to pinpoint which format is doing the best on any topic you want to cover.

Cons

While BuzzSumo can certainly give your content a massive boost, it's not a stand-alone content management system. You'll still need a CMS to meet the full scope of your content planning, creation and distribution needs. Smaller complaints include minor quirks, such as the inability to dive deeper into certain statistics. The system can provide you with alerts for the minimum number of shares content received on social networks, for instance, but it won't break those numbers down by specific site. It also ranks influencers based solely on their Twitter reputations, without taking other background or factors into play.

Convert

convert.com
Easy experiments at your fingertips

Convert is a testing platform that allows you to set up unlimited experiments using three different testing types on your website. Test choices include the standard A/B test, which compares two or more different versions of a page against the original; the split-URL experiment, which compares results from two different pages you have already created; and multivariate experiments, which allow you to test two or more different items on a page against each other to find the most effective combination of elements.

The A/B testing feature is the platform's highlight, and it lets clients test website changes in real time to see how the changes affect performance and eventual conversion rates. The platform is used by a notable array of some of the world's largest corporations and organizations, including Sony, Kmart and UNICEF. Convert can also easily be integrated into a variety of different services that clients may already be using, including Bitium, CallRail, Drupal, CallFire, Google Analytics and others.

Pros

Ease-of-use tops Convert's benefits list. Very little information technology involvement is necessary, as you need only install a single snippet of JavaScript code on your site to get the platform up and running. A visual editor tool pops up, guiding you through the process of setting up and launching your testing experiments. Convert also lets you measure many different factors, all of which go into determining the ultimate performance of a finished site. You can set up an unlimited number of performance-related goals, for example, and then test each one to measure the individual impact it's having on the site. You'll receive insights on JavaScript events, clicks, mouseovers and other behaviors, allowing you to see how certain changes are affecting website interaction.

Cons

Perhaps the only major limitation of Convert is the fact that it is only an A/B and multivariate testing platform and offers little else in the way of functionality. Other platforms that provide the same levels of reporting and testing capabilities as Convert also provide additional functionalities that help ensure users get everything they need from a single platform.

Although Convert doesn't come with additional functions, it does come with the ability to integrate with a wide range of services. As long as you're willing to integrate Convert into your existing infrastructure and aren't looking for a be-all, end-all optimization platform, the service can be a handy one.

Grammarbase

grammarbase.com
Real, live proofreading and editing pros

Automated spelling and grammar checks can be a godsend for quickly correcting glaring errors, but that doesn't mean they don't leave a few errors of their own in their wake, such as "they're" versus "their" or "lets" versus "let's." Sometimes they leave you with sentences that are grammatically correct yet make no earthly sense. Such mistakes can drop your site's credibility and make you the laughingstock of online grammar geeks.

Grammarbase can help. Unlike automated checks, Grammarbase puts your content in front of real, live proofreaders and editors. All are certifiable pros, hired according to industry standards and heavily vetted with extensive exams before they're invited to join the team. Simply paste your text or upload your document to the site and receive a proofread and edited document emailed back to you in as few as three hours.

Pros

Grammarbase gives you a double dose of professional help with a two-editor system to ensure flawless results. If you're in a massive rush, you can opt for an urgent order and get it back in as few as three hours. The standard service provides proofreading and editing, but you can request proofreading only, checking of your entire website, or other customized services to suit your exact proofreading and editing needs. The service runs around the clock, making it perfect for those last-minute, 3 a.m. blog posts.

Cons

Real, live people will be viewing your content, which can give pause to those with top-secret content they won't even let their own mothers see. You'll also receive results in the form of a Microsoft Word document, with edits noted in the Track Changes feature. While Word users will have no problem with this, those who wish to convert the file into another format may end up with issues due to the tracked changes.

Grammarly

grammarly.com
Ironing out mistakes

Grammarly's free writing app ensures that everything you type is easy to read, effective, and mistake-free. As you type, Grammarly will underline any spelling or grammatical errors and help you fix them on the fly. It works in your browser and in Windows versions of Microsoft Word and Outlook.

Pros

Grammarly is generally more powerful than the built-in spelling and grammar checkers in most word processing systems. It also comes equipped with a plagiarism checker to help ensure your content is truly unique. Additional perks include the contextual spell checker and vocabulary enhancement tool. The contextual spell checker looks at the words surrounding an identified mistake to ensure that it wasn't intentional and that you're using the proper word. The vocabulary enhancement feature continuously makes suggestions about word choice, helping to ensure that you're using the most powerful and effective words to get your point across.

Cons

The free checker lets you paste your text right into the text box on the platform but then teases you by requiring you to set up an account with your email address before it will hand over the results. Some have complained that their free trials turned into automatic subscription plans, which they were unable to easily cancel. As is the case with some grammar checkers, Grammarly has been known to be a tad overzealous, pinpointing errors where there are none or making superfluous suggestions. Grammarly could be an ideal tool for non-native English speakers or others who fall prey to common grammatical mistakes but might be more of a nuisance to those with a firm command of the English language who are writing more advanced copy.

HubSpot

hubspot.com
All-in-one spot for content marketing

Content is the currency of modern marketing, but to drive revenue for your business content needs to be well planned, optimized and measured. That's hard to do with a dozen fragmented tools. HubSpot is an all-in-one inbound marketing system that helps you create content to attract visitors and convert them into happy leads and customers. Each content tool within HubSpot includes as-you-type search engine optimization, responsive design for mobile devices, a dynamic personalization engine, and detailed analytics on performance. Plus, because HubSpot is rooted in a contact database, you'll know who is reading your content and where they are in their purchase decision. Since its 2006 debut, the platform has amassed more than 18,000 users in 90 countries. HubSpot's complete offerings include a marketing platform, a free CRM, and a collection of sales enablement tools. Three pricing plans give you specific features with each tier. You can get the CRM for free and try the marketing platform free for 30 days.

Pros

The interconnected nature of HubSpot transforms all the pieces of your content marketing puzzle into a cohesive whole. The SEO tools are a prime example, with other platforms often forcing you to do keyword research elsewhere and then import or transfer the results. Not so with HubSpot. Here your SEO suggestions remain visible alongside your content tools. Blogging software provides as-you-type instructions for improving your content without add-ons or plug-ins.

Social media tools let you plug into your contact database, color-coding all your leads and customers for quick identification when they visit your social media sites. Landing pages can be tweaked to show visitors content based on their interests. Email marketing tools let you build campaigns right from the platform. Did we mention you also get up-to-the-minute marketing data on the activity of your leads? Not all features come with all pricing tiers.

Cons

It's a good thing that HubSpot's interface is easy to use and its learning curve fairly small, since you have to pay extra for any technical support. This support fee can be a hefty one to get HubSpot operational if you're not experienced in coding. The overall initial investment to get the platform up and running can be a deal breaker, especially when you realize you can find the same types of tools at a lower cost or even for free elsewhere. What you're paying for is the supreme convenience of having them integrated all in one spot.

InboundWriter

inboundwriter.com
Near magical predictions

Remember that Magic 8 Ball toy that you'd shake to get a magical answer about the future? InboundWriter kind of works like that, giving you seemingly magical answers about content you intend to write. The easy-to-use platform lets you input the topic you intend to write about, and then it serves up a host of answers on how that content is expected to perform. It researches your content idea, tells you if it's good one or a bomb, suggests ideas that might work better, and even gives you tips on how to go about creating the content. All this good stuff is generated by algorithms driven by real-time analytical data that comes from keeping an eye on how people behave and consume content online. Predictions and recommendations are also regularly back-tested to ensure they're staying on the mark.

Pros

Although a number of other platforms may serve up data and statistics that can help you plan your content, they typically hand over a bunch of numbers and tell you to go figure out the rest on your own. InboundWriter does all the figuring for you, giving you straightforward guidance and suggestions on how you can specifically improve your ideas to create top-notch content. It can specifically isolate which elements of a piece may negatively affect performance and which sites would be best suited for a specific piece of content while providing real-time results on keywords that reflect the daily changes in the online world.

Cons

InboundWriter can serve up very useful predictions — as long as you give it ideas and topics it can compute. Anyone feeding ideas to InboundWriter must have at least a basic knowledge of search engine optimization in order to choose useful terms with which the platform can work. The number of documents you can optimize per month is extremely limited. The free version only lets you optimize four documents each month whereas the professional plan allows you 15 documents per month for a monthly fee of about $50.

Influitive AdvocateHub

influitive.com
Referral marketing solution for B2B

AdvocateHub offers B2B companies a way to turbo-charge their marketing efforts by building communities of brand advocates and happy customers. Influitive invites participants in these communities to complete challenges that enhance the brand like doing reviews, making reference calls or offering referrals. Each completed challenge provides points that go towards badges they can use for a variety of perks.

Through AdvocateHub, you utilize your best asset to promote your brand – word of mouth. Studies show that referral leads are 10 to 20 times more valuable than direct sales or inbound web leads. The problem with most referral systems is they still require manual campaigns that are often poorly targeted or ill-timed. AdvocateHub takes the guesswork out of the process, so B2B businesses get the most from their referral system.

Add to this formula ease of use and you'll find Influitive's product is a winner. AdvocateHub is available 24/7 through a web portal, an integrated website tool or a mobile app. This program is tightly integrated with Saleforce.com, as well, so there is full visibility for your sales and marketing teams.

Pros
Gives new meaning to the term multitask. With AdvocateHub, you can do tackle multiple tasks at once with minimum effort. The goal here is to create communities, so you can work in groups without less repetition and redundancy. The marketing assets coming from this program look more personalized and tailored, too, making this a better option than mass email programs.
The company gets top marks for customer service, as well. They realize AdvocateHub is a work in progress and are open to making improvements based on feedback.

Cons
Influitive is still working out some of the bugs. There are reports of the program being unstable at times. Most glitches resolve themselves

quickly. It also takes some time to check on the current challenges and to fill point rewards.

Keyword Tool
keywordtool.io
Starting place for keyword selection

Optimizing your content is meant to improve your traffic, not create stress and extra expenses. Keyword tool takes advantage of Google's own autocomplete capabilities to automatically generate up to 750 long-tailed keywords for free. Avoid the guesswork in developing keyword strategies by figuring out the most popular search terms without the hassle of logging into Google AdWords.

Pros
Keyword Tool searches for relevant keywords on Google, YouTube, Bing, Amazon and Google Play. Set your search criteria to focus on international, national or state trends online, making your keyword selection relevant. Keyword Tool supports API integration, and a subscription to Keyword Tool Pro expands the tool's capabilities. You can also search for CPC-specific keywords and keyword variants among your competitors within Google AdWords within the tool as well.

Pro subscriptions are available in three tiers. Pro Basic and Pro Plus double the search volume and number of keywords compiled. Pro Keyword Tool allows users to pay for subscriptions on a monthly basis, which is practically unheard of in content optimization.

Cons
Keyword Tool Pro is best for those with experience in keyword strategies. If you are just starting to develop your content strategy, you may need to hire a consultant to help figure out what direction to take. Searching through Keyword Tool could easily lead to hours of work, and that does not even begin to tackle content creation. Trials of Pro subscriptions in Keyword Tool are unavailable, but the company does offer a 30-day money back guarantee. Moreover, the level of customer support is determined by the level of the purchased subscription.

Klout

klout.com
Social media superpower

Klout is a website and mobile app that lets you peek under the hood of the social media engine. Klout creates a score based on critical factors that represent your influence in that virtual world. The score ranges from 1 to 100 – the more influential you are the higher the mark. Based on that information, you know if you need to work harder at networking and step your expertise or whether you are right on track with your social media plan.

Klout also offers suggestions that help improve your standing. It shows you shareable content that your followers have yet to see. It helps you produce information that matters to the people that read your content and it monitors retweets, likes and shares to help you improve your posting power.retweets, likes and shares to help you improve your posting power.

Pros

If your business goal this year involves enhancing your social media presence, Klout is an essential tool to have in your arsenal. You see at a glance the impact you make with each posting, tweet or discussion. The program helps you provide information that people really look for as opposed to making you guess what to post next.

Cons

There has been some criticism about this product's methodology. The Klout scores for mainstream social media influencers are confusing and inaccurate, according to some experts. Some of them believe the program puts too much emphasis on powerful connections no matter who they are or whether they relate to a business. A Klout score of 80 might simply mean you have some powerful people with a high number of followers that monitor your posts. It doesn't mean that they share any of them. The keyword search just returns a list of accounts with that word or phrase. It does not tell you who is influential in a category or silo.

Kred

home.kred

See your visual stream

Kred is about measuring influence via a visual stream. Every post, comment and tweet creates a ripple that is almost visual. With that in mind, Kred measures the impact you have on the Internet river – giving you what you need to become more influential.

Kred focuses on two key platforms: Twitter and Facebook. By analyzing billions of tweets, this system is able to make connections that stick. The process allows you to see who the main influencers are in any sector and where you stand on that list. When you know who is making the largest ripples, you can utilize that information to galvanize your own impact. Kred create communities focused on trends, so brands and influencers make connections.

Kred does more than just measure influence, though. It estimates the outreach, as well. A high Kred score means the person engages with others often by sharing, replying or following other accounts.

Pros

Kred looks at specific data points to determine a score. This metric system goes beyond just the number of followers and shares an account gets. It focuses on the activity offered by the account holder, as well. That puts it above other tools like Klout that have a limited reach.

When looking at your own influence, Kred offers a more data points to consider, as well. You see a 30-day follower graph and a list of influences you have had within the social media community.

Cons

It is almost too much information to interpret. The dashboard for this program looks chaotic. Not every name that pops up is really an influencer, either. For example, you might do a search for "writers" and get Richard Branson at the top of the list. While Richard Branson is a writer, he's not an exact fit for that search category.

Leadpages

Leadpages.net
Hosting and distribution rolled into one

Leadpages is a comprehensive content marketing tool, and it revolves around the use of free materials to encourage visitors to join your email list. Leadpages also allows you to select from hundreds of templates to create custom landing pages in minutes. Consequently, Leadpages stands out as one of the best-integrated content marketing platforms currently in existence.

Pros

All templates on Leadpages are designed with mobile in mind. Designing custom landing pages is made even simpler through the use of drag-and-drop tools, and Leadpages hosts a variety of analytics capabilities. The focus of Leadpages is on growing leads and distributing your content. Ultimately, a customer who signs up for your newsletters or emails is more likely to convert to a paying customer if you provide something enticing.

Leadpages also offers dedicated support specialists through email, chat, or phone. It integrates easily with WordPress through a simple plugin, and functions on an unlimited number of domains. Leadpages seamlessly integrates with major CRM tools, such as Infusionsoft, Zoho and Salesforce, e-commerce solutions, email distribution providers like AWeber and Constant Contact, and other advertising platforms. Additional integrations of Leadpages include Facebook Ads and Google AdWords.

Cons

When created, Leadpages did not have drag-and-drop capabilities, so many businesses and marketers avoided the platform. Unlike the majority of content management tools, Leadpages does not offer a free trial, and all initial subscriptions must be paid. However, you have the option to cancel within 30 days for a full refund. Leadpages is also unable to accept PayPal for purchases.

When it comes to customer service and support, the minimal subscription only includes email support. The medium subscription includes email and live chat support. Only the largest subscription, which costs approximately $2,400 annually, supports email, chat and phone customer service.

Majestic

majestic.com
Backlink magic

Majestic is a specialist search engine and one of the largest web crawlers on the planet after Google and Bing. Majestic is a search engine like no other. Instead of indexing "content", the search engine monitors and analyses the links between web pages to derive both the Trust and the context of every page and domain on the web. Their "Trust Flow" metrics have become one of the mainstay measurements for SEOs, Domainers and Content Marketers alike as a universal way to compare pages and sites across the web. Because Majestic has its own index of the Internet, their algorithms and data is not prone to being removed or overly affected by third parties. Over time, this has helped Majestic to become a "must have" power house tool for Internet Marketers. Whilst a free version is available, the real power cuts in from around $50 a month.

Pros
Majestic makes backlink reporting a breeze, thanks to out-of-the box reporting with a user-friendly interface for all the basic functions. You can download information and create custom analysis and reporting while enjoying instant access to link information about your site. Useful summaries give your link-building strategies an additional boost. Flexible subscription options and pricing plans make it cost-effective, enabling you to pay only for the features you intend to use. Each plan comes with a limited number of downloads each month.

Cons
Although the powerful data tool gives you an equally powerful edge for backlink strategies, it doesn't offer a lot of other SEO-related functionality. It may also be difficult to interpret some of the charts and graphs, especially without in-depth knowledge. The same holds true for other data delivery formats, which are geared for analysis by experts rather than newbies. Even experts may find it takes longer

to make the most of the data provided by Majestic than the data obtained from some other tools. The Majestic tool also lacks an easy way to compare site backlinks with performance on competitor sites. Another con, albeit small, is the requirement of PayPal payments to be made in British pounds.

Moz

moz.com
Optimization gold mine

Moz is a veritable one-stop shop for numerous search engine and content optimization needs. The suite of tools included in the Pro subscription includes the backbone of Moz analytics, along with a Web explorer that discovers link-building opportunities, a rank tracker that fills you in on page and domain ranks for any given keyword, an on-page grader for keyword usage, keyword difficulty rankings and a crawl test. Moz not only provides analytical results, but it also serves up useful suggestions that help you identify website errors, missed conversions and areas where search engine optimization could be improved. And the platform is not done yet. The site provides a steady supply of useful blog posts, along with custom reports, research tools and a thriving Q&A community.

Pros
Moz is hailed by industry experts for setting the gold standard for optimization tools. Extensive analysis identifies site weaknesses, giving webmasters a clear roadmap for improvement for sites of any size or scope. You can request customized reports that meet your specific requirements, while the Moz SEO toolbar gives you a summarized view of all your tracking and reports to easily keep tabs on the success of content optimization efforts. Strong customer support comes from the in-depth blog, various guidebooks and a dependable customer service department that is available via email, phone or live chat. Moz has continuously improved over the years, with regularly updated apps that remain easy to install and use. Moz even offers free apps that you can try out on your site.

Cons

Limited keyword tracking is a common complaint, with the number of keyword rankings you can track depending on the version of Moz you pay for. This is an especially loud complaint since some competitors offer unlimited keyword tracking with all of their services. Other limits are placed on the number of campaigns, page crawls and competitor comparisons you can run on a monthly basis. Slow updates produce another groan, with rating and crawl statistics updated weekly. Although the updates create consistency, the slow rate doesn't appeal to those interested in immediate numbers or statistics.

Optimizely

optimizely.com
User experience mastermind

Even if your website looks amazing with its fabulous user interface, it can still be turnoff if it delivers a poor user experience. Optimizely focuses on enhancing the user experience side of things, helping to ensure that all elements on your website, mobile app or platform work together to form a cohesive whole. This platform gives you a solid foundation for creating the best possible customer experience by delivering real-time, actionable data you can use to improve your site's function and feel.

Pros

Easy integration tops the list of benefits, with Optimizely ready for action by inserting a single line of HTML into your website or platform. The Optimizely interface then treats you to huge amounts of actionable data regarding your site's performance, including clicks, conversions, signups and more. Your job is to use the data to increase engagement levels, optimize interactions and boost total conversions, which all lead back to higher return on investment.

If you're not sure what changes to make to improve your ROI, Optimizely lets you perform A/B and other multivariate testing. Run these tests as you wish, using features that let you schedule them for a future date and allocate traffic to tests to compare the existing version of your site to the updated one. One more plus is the ability to target optimized experiences based on demographic, app version, device type, referral URL, traffic source and other audience conditions.

Cons

Although Optimizely easily integrates into your own platform or site, it can get pretty finicky when it comes to integrating with other services you may be using. If you're looking to integrate Optimizely with your existing analytics service, for example, it's important to know that it only works with three: Google Analytics, KISSmetrics and Mixpanel. While this may not be a problem if you are indeed using one of the chosen three, additional platform compatibility would be welcome.

SEMrush

semrush.com
Super-charged keyword tool

You have your typical keyword search tools — and then you have SEMrush. This Web-based search engine optimization tool gathers enormous amounts of search engine results page data for up to 500 keywords across five of your campaigns, filling you in on the small details that can make a huge difference for your optimization strategies. The tool analyzes high-ranking domains for specific search terms and generates a list of keywords, including synonyms and variations, to produce a seemingly endless list of keywords to add to your pool. Get an even more powerful edge with suggestions for keyword expressions and long-tail keywords, the latter of which make up 70 percent of all search traffic and face less competition than single-word options.

International businesses will appreciate SEMrush's ability to get regional keywords to target audiences across the globe. SEMrush has a 26-country regional database, including Mexico, Canada, the United States, the United Kingdom and Hong Kong. For those with multilingual websites, keyword research can be done in 16 languages.

Pros

SEMrush is an advanced tool for advanced keyword research analysis. It works to improve organic keyword rankings, learn competitors' top keywords, identify high-ranking keywords, find low-competition keywords, and identify profitable keywords for content and landing pages. It also has a live update algorithm to refresh its regional databases. The popularity and search volume is updated daily, weekly or monthly. It also has awesome tools, such as site audit, keyword difficulty, domain vs. domain comparison, and position tracking. All around, SEMrush digs deep. Along with identifying effective keywords for content, it lets you know what your competition's top keywords are. It's like having your own online detective.

Cons

One of the cons of SEMrush is lack of speed. The search bar option runs slowly at times, requiring you to refresh to find specific keywords. Another downside is that the tool doesn't distinguish between organic and local listings, and you can't track rankings separately in Yahoo and Bing — the keyword rank provided could apply to either one. Users have also recommended that SEMrush be updated with the ability to duplicate campaigns. This addition would make tracking across multiple areas much easier.

SiteTuners

sitetuners.com
Evidence-based optimization and testing

Your online persona speaks volumes about your company. Poorly written or designed websites can become ghosts in today's advanced algorithms in Google and Bing. When your success hinges on your optimization skills, SiteTuners offers a way to review your website, recommend changes, and test such changes in a fast, efficient manner. The focus of SiteTuners is content strategy, and small to large businesses can take advantage of the platform's experts in conversion optimization. SiteTuners has gained additional notoriety for hosting the international Conversion Conference over the last decade.

Pros

SiteTuners is built on website optimization, landing page testing and conversion management. Have your website reviewed in 45- or 90-minute increments at a predetermined rate of $699 and $1,099 respectively. If your site needs recurring review and insight, SiteTuners offers a monthly subscription to Ongoing Conversion Support. Reviews are also available on landing pages or entire sites, making this tool perfect for minor to major changes in your content strategy. SiteTuners offers an array of freebies to help you along the way, such as webinars, podcasts and blog posts.

Cons

SiteTuners touches on the importance of analytics and A/B testing, but you cannot receive detailed breakdown of what you get with each payment beyond a quick list. SiteTuners is not built for small businesses that generate less than $1 million, which makes many startups incapable of accessing the service.

Some of the benefits of using SiteTuners are simply using other content tools as well. For example, one of the key perks of an express review is an AttentionWizard heatmap. However, the cost of this heatmap is only $27 for smaller websites. Furthermore, SiteTuners does not actually create content, so you will need to create content that aligns with the site's recommendations. While SiteTuners may be a viable option for medium-sized businesses, small businesses with less than $500,000 annually may benefit from using multiple, less expensive tools to get similar results.

Smartling
smartling.com
For smart translations

Since 2009, Smartling has been the go-to company to translate and localize content, even back when their office was a coffee shop in Manhattan. It is safe to say this tech startup has grown a lot since those coffee-infused days. The company just recently acquired Jargon on Crunchbase to expand their market to include mobile developers looking to localize internationally.

With Smartling, you gain access to a global fluency platform that allows brands to translate content as it is created. This eliminated 90 percent of the manual effort associated with translation and localization. The goal is to eliminate errors and ambiguities via the in-context translation and review toolset.Smartling, you gain access to a global fluency platform that allows brands to translate content as it is created. This eliminated 90 percent of the manual effort associated with translation and localization. The goal is to eliminate errors and ambiguities via the in-context translation and review toolset.

In addition, brands can leverage their existing transitions in a centralized repository, so future translations are fast, accurate and consistent. With global brand consistency, you guarantee native experiences across all brand touchpoints, taking your business international cleanly and professionally. Smartling works with mainstream global companies such as Spotify, TNT and Pinterest. touchpoints, taking your business international cleanly and professionally. Smartling works with mainstream global companies such as Spotify, TNT and Pinterest.Smartling works with mainstream global companies such as Spotify, TNT and Pinterest. Smartling is fully web-based, so you have access to it at any time and with any operating system.

Pros

The platform is easy to learn and very intuitive. There are no time-consuming training sessions because the features are straightforward and user-friendly. With this one system, you have access to essential tools such as a glossary, translation guide and in-context translation. There is a comments section that allows you to ask questions and get a quick response.

Cons

For the most part, users report a positive experience with this service. At least one reviewer complained the design structure slows him down. If a 100 percent match is found by the translation management tool, is does not fully propagated, making you call up each translation for review. A few users stated the platform is occasionally buggy, as well.

Sniply

snip.ly

Transform social media posts into CTAs

Social media is great, but you still need to hope the customer heads to your website or page. Stop worrying about if visitors will convert by using Sniply. This content optimization tool empowers simple posts by turning them into actionable devices for newsletter subscriptions, requests for more information and more. Of course, creating a CTA button, text, form or image, otherwise known as a "Snip," is only part of the tool's perks. Depending on the level of your account, you can create brands that do not have Sniply advertising watermarks and track every action a visitor takes through analytics within the "Snip."

Pros

Customization is critical in keeping your visitors engaged and on target. "Snips" are entirely customizable, and you can get started by using an existing theme. If you subscribe to higher tiers of service, you will get additional clicks and a free domain. Pro subscribers can take advantage of retargeting pixels to help lost visitors return to their site. Similar to Bitly, each "Snip" includes a custom shortlink without the hassle of visiting other sites. Sniply is capable of full integration with existing applications, such as Hootsuite, Sendible, Mailchimp and Zapier, and extensions are available for Chrome, Safari, Firefox and Explorer.

Cons

Users of Sniply may not understand the difference between clicks and "Snips," leading to disappointment and lost investments. Each plan limits the number of clicks per month, and businesses or enterprises with more than five team members will need to sign up for an Enterprise Plan, which range in cost from $299 to $2,000 monthly.

SpyFu

spyfu.com
Toppling competitors, one at a time

An easy interface combined with a continuously growing catalog of advantages makes SpyFu a top contender in the world of search marketing research and tracking software. SpyFu's main claim to fame is its ability to essentially spy on your competitors, researching their keywords, ad variations and organic rankings to expose their search marketing secret formulas. The platform then helps you topple those same competitors by arming you with the information you need to restructure your own pay-per-click accounts, design new paid and organic search initiatives, and generate more leads.

Pros

Deep details on your competition shoot SpyFu to the top of the list for tracking and research software. The Kombat Tool lets you view your competition's keywords and ad copy, glimpsing which content brings in the highest returns. You can also check which ads your competition has been running the longest as well as the keywords that hold the highest bids. Further information includes Web-specific data on your competitors' sites, such as the number of incoming links, the number of daily clicks, and website load time.

You can find and use competitor domain names as keywords, download all organic keywords and AdWords, and review 200 of your competitors' highest-priced AdSense keywords. The platform also offers an organic search engine optimization dashboard to track how well your website is performing, along with suggestions on higher impact keywords and competitors you should track. All this data adds up to valuable ammunition for revamping and optimizing your own campaigns.

Cons

Although SpyFu is compatible with Google, the software is unable to offer PPC insight for Yahoo or Bing. The platform can sometimes be less than accurate when it comes to keywords and ad positions. SpyFu also lacks a place to edit the AdWords in your own campaign; neither does it offer the ability to host a SpyFu white-label dashboard on your own domain.

SumoMe

sumome.com
Fast development without coding knowledge

SumoMe is an incredibly easy tool to use and install for increasing the performance and optimization of your website. After creating a free account, copy and paste a generated code into your website before <body> tags. A guided tutorial teaches you how to use the system. Instantly monitor traffic, connect to Google Analytics by signing into your Google account, install free SumoMe Analytics, create an e-commerce store, and more with the press of a button, similar to clicking an app in your phone.

Pros
Capabilities in SumoMe range from heatmaps to form generation. Never worry about complicated form-processing scripts again with this tool. The cost of using the platform is based on the number of clicks you have, not the number of services you want. Each subscription includes 11 apps and individual apps are entirely customizable to your needs. Create responsive navigation bars quickly, and link your SumoMe-created e-store to the payment processing platform, Stripe. If you have not signed up for Stripe, SumoMe can take care of that as well. Everything is processed through SumoMe, reducing workload and increasing traffic to your site.

Cons
SumoMe can be costly if your site has a high volume of traffic, approximately $399 monthly. The price climbs if you purchase SumoMe on a monthly basis, which is ill-advised for e-commerce sites. If you fail to renew your subscription, your buttons lose their functionality, and you could lose your entire investment in a moment. However, you can sign up for a free trial on any of the plans with a credit card. You must cancel your account before the renewal date, or you will be charged the full amount, which is nonrefundable.

Unbounce

unbounce.com
Conversion simplified and IT-proof landing pages

Playing on the concept of a visitor who "bounces" off a displeasing landing page, Unbounce is one of the best resources for creating high-quality landing pages for all of your marketing campaign needs. Depending on your subscription type, you can take advantage of pay-per-click advertising, complete CRM integration and analytics.

Pros

Unbounce offers custom landing pages and eliminates problems that routinely arise in internal information technology departments when creating landing pages. Unbounce offers up to 78 customizable templates to start the creation process. If you dislike the existing templates, you can choose to upload templates from ThemeForest or Convert Themes.

Landing pages automatically snap to the size of visitors' devices, which strengthens search engine ranking, and the platform's capabilities include dynamic text. As a result, your landing page stays relevant to the changing mindsets of prospective visitors. You may change subscription plans at any time, which is essential to your organization's scalability. Unbounce further heightens a visitor's experience by allowing you to create custom forms and interactive features in a drag-and-drop environment.

Cons

The most significant drawback to using Unbounce is price. Compared to many other content optimization and creation tools, Unbounce is more expensive. For example, Pro 199 subscriptions to Unbounce cost $199 monthly. Regardless of which subscription is selected, all Unbounce subscriptions comprise only one custom domain. For businesses seeking to capitalize on similar domain names, Unbounce is an illogical choice. Furthermore, Unbounce imposes limitations of between 5,000 and 100,000 unique visitors to your landing page.

Visual Website Optimizer

vwo.com

A/B testing as easy as ABC

Billed as the world's easiest A/B testing tool, Visual Website Optimizer might just live up to its status, thanks to a wide range of features delivered in a single, user-friendly platform. In a few swift moves, you can set up various tests for landing pages, websites, e-commerce pages and other elements, tracking the ways users interact with those elements as well as each element's eventual performance. Feel free to play around with changes as drastic as a major graphical overhaul on a landing page, instantly implementing and pushing out the change to a select segment of your Web traffic. Visual Website Optimizer lets you compare the performance of your updated page with the original in real time, pinpointing which elements work, which don't, and where you can focus strategic adjustments.

Pros

Easy-to-follow visuals are the main strength of this platform, allowing you to track changes and ongoing tests at a glance. The dashboard compiles a host of useful information on a single screen, including the current version of your page as well as all its design enhancements over a designated period of time. Dashboard statistics additionally update in real time, allowing you to take immediate note of elements that work — and even more immediate action on those that fail. Easy installation is another major benefit. Simply paste a single line of code into your site, and you're in. Your site will then have access to the main dashboard, where you can control all the functions and features you wish to use.

Cons

Complaints have surfaced about the editing tool, which has been described as finicky and requiring the coding of some elements for the testing variation to function properly. The variation preview feature has been known to fail, making users turn back to the editor to preview their variations. Some data tends to fall between the cracks after a test is completed and stopped, requiring users to document test results outside of the platform if they want to ensure accuracy.

Wordstream

Wordstream.com
Keyword tool with muscle for customized PPC and more

Wordstream is a robust keyword planning and SEO optimization tool that lets you manage paid search and paid social campaigns using a single interface. The central feature of Wordstream is its Advisor tool, developed to help content managers create and optimize content, then measure and optimize your content for high-performing and highly customized PPC campaigns.

Wordstream also offers visual reports in an easy-to-digest format as well as landing page and call-tracking tools and a dedicated team to help them make the most of all the product's features based on the subscriber's unique needs. Optimized "smart alerts" help content managers optimize content based on the latest trends to make the most of their advertising budgets, and there are three subscription levels to suit businesses of all sizes. In addition to its paid services, Wordstream offers four free tools - a keyword tool, a keyword niche finder, a keyword grouper and – especially helpful – a negative keyword tool - to get a taste of Wordstream's capabilities without ponying up for a paid subscription.

Pros

In addition to the free tools, Wordstream offers continuous keyword analysis and discovery, which can be a huge boon to busy business owners, marketing agencies and content strategists who dread the thought of poring over detailed analytics reports to identify new keywords to target. Wordstream uses real-time access to Google Analytics to automatically harvest new keywords, which it then sends to your Wordstream keyword database. The Create SEO Content plugin suggests variations of keywords are you're composing your content, and it's compatible with WordPress, Blogger, Drupal and other major CMS platforms.

Cons

As a keyword and PPC optimizer, Wordstream offers plenty of advantages, but for businesses looking for more than that – like a complete SEO suite – Wordstream probably will not be a good fit. Wordstream doesn't offer comprehensive site auditing or an in-depth competitive analysis of keywords, and for sites light on content, Wordstream won't be used to its best advantage.

Wordtracker
wordtracker.com
Tons of prime keywords

In-depth keyword research has been the name of the game for Wordtracker since 1998. Online marketers can use this convenient tool to discover prime keywords that people are using in searches, along with a rundown on the number of websites that are stocked with those particular words. Such information is a boon for marketers looking to optimize content in the hopes of increasing search engine traffic.

You can type in any word or phrase and then view lists of related search queries. If you own a website that specializes in duct tape, for instance, you might enter the phrase "duct tape." Wordtracker jumps into action, revealing related searches such as "duct tape wallet design" and "duct tape Christmas gifts." In addition to revealing search volume, Wordtracker fills you in on how many Web pages use a keyword or have inbound links with the term in their anchor text.

Pros
One of Wordtracker's top benefits is serving up detailed global search data collected from multiple sources. It calculates and lists a keyword effectiveness rating for each query, which can help you quickly identify phrases that will give you the most bang for your buck. For most queries, it can provide more than 200 related terms and their rankings, opening the door to options you may not have even considered. You can access the data on either the Wordtracker website or via a Chrome browser extension, and new users get a free trial to give the tool a whirl. The free trial lasts seven days and includes all features provided in a paid subscription. You can also get a quick sample of Wordtracker data by entering a keyword in the search box on its homepage.

Cons

Make the most of the free trial, as paid subscriptions come with a substantial monthly or annual fee. But the comprehensive data Wordtracker provides is far superior to free alternatives, and it does charge lower rates than similar tools, such as Keyword Discovery. Occasional complaints about downtime and other problems pop up on forums, and technical support is only offered during normal U.K. business hours. The overall accuracy of Wordtracker statistics is another sticking point. Automated computer software and small groups still have the potential to skew this data. For example, an obscure keyword could end up appearing to be fairly popular just because three individuals tirelessly search for it every day.

Wordy

wordy.com
Add the human touch to your editing

There are plenty of apps out there that promise to correct spelling and grammar, but nothing says professional like the human touch. That is what the real-time editing service Wordy offers customers. Wordy is about having a pair of human eyes look at your copy and eradicating those little errors that both you and the app miss. Wordy promises to optimize your content for both accuracy and readability.

The editors working with this company are well-vetted and continually tested to ensure they are at the top of their game. The editors are also native language speakers, so you get the best possible editing solution.

At Wordy, the editors work on your schedule, not the other way around. There are editors available in all major time zones, so you have 24/7 editing at your disposal. They also work in all major file formats including Microsoft Office, PDF's, LaTeX and rich text files. Wordy service is available Google Docs, as well. You choose the service you want for this company, too. They offer proofreading, copy-editing or a combined effort for both. The pricing scheme is based on per-word plans.

Pros

The human touch means you don't have to deal with those silly autocorrect issues that you get with some grammar apps. The real-time editing by real editor also means you are getting access to all the current rules and standards regardless of the style. The editors are well-versed in academic writing, API and Chicago styles and different types of citations and footnotes.

Cons

You can use most apps for free although some have limitations. There is no free service available from Wordy. They offer real editors, not an algorithm and that type of attention costs money.

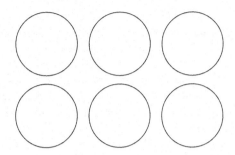

Content Distribution

Tools for marketing automation,
curation, promotion, social media
platforms, email marketing, and PPC

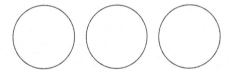

Act-On

act-on.com
Big-time automation for smaller businesses

Smaller and medium-sized businesses that crave but typically can't afford big-time marketing automation platforms now have an alternative. Its name is Act-On, and it's a powerful distribution platform that lets you automate and track both inbound and outbound marketing strategies. Act-On serves up a cache of tools that streamline all the best campaign management strategies, such as lead nurturing, lead scoring, list management, customer relationship management integration, and automated programs. Unlike larger, more complex options that can often take weeks or months to set up, Act-On promises that most businesses can get the platform up and running in a single day. The dashboard can be customized to integrate key features you intend to use, so Act-On conforms to the needs of your business instead of the other way around.

Pros
Act-On has indeed been hailed as incredibly easy to use, without the steep learning curve, information technology involvement, or special knowledge required for many similar software programs. An attractive graphical user interface lets you easily manage and optimize all aspects of the customer experience. You're also able to track and compare your marketing spending on various channels, letting you see which are thriving and which could use a bit of a boost. Additional tracking capabilities apply to the activity of your leads, showcasing behaviors that include the initial point of engagement, the conversion point, the moment the sale closed, and the frequency at which first-time customers are turning into repeat business.

Cons
The software is designed for medium-sized and smaller businesses, and the pricing structure appears designed to essentially punish you if you grow beyond that scope. Your cost for using the platform is heavily dependent on the total number of active contacts with which your site interacts, with an active contact defined as any contact in your database that gets a monthly email from the system. Start out with 1,000 active contacts, and you'll pay $600 per month, billed annually. But if you increase your contacts to 2,500 or 5,000, your price

jumps to $750 or $900 per month, billed annually. An annual contract is also required, with your monthly fee subject to change if your business amasses additional active contacts.

Bounce Exchange
Bounceexchange.com
Optimize conversions with behavioral-based automation

Bounce Exchange bills itself as a "behavioral automation platform" that helps companies build leads and improve and optimize conversions by reacting to site visitors' "digital body language," or engagement behaviors exhibited on your site. Bounce Exchange is well-known for its proprietary exit-intent technology that tracks and measures real-time factors like mouse movement and speed and even cursor location to enable businesses to launch "hyper-targeted" marketing initiatives aimed at turning casual visitors into subscribers and customers. For instance, when a visitor's mouse breaks the browser plane and approaches the address bar, Bounce Exchange can be used to deploy campaigns like pop-ups to stimulate visitors to become subscribers or to offer incentives like coupons or free downloadable deliverables. It sounds simple, but the algorithms used to measure visitors' real-time data are continually evolving to provide a more robust and interactive experience for visitors and improved conversion rates for businesses that use Bounce Exchange.

Pros
Bounce Exchange is arguably the most visible and most well-known player in the exit intent technology arena, with huge companies buying into their platform and using it in their own marketing initiatives. As a result, your company can tap into the leaders in exit intent strategy and technology and capitalize on the past successes (and mistakes) of leading brands. Exit intent strategies can be customized for your company and "taught" to evolve over time to optimize conversions even as site visitor habits change.

Cons
Some visitors may find the automatic launch of marketing initiatives to be annoying, so knowing your target audience and using pop-ups

judiciously and only on pages most likely to convert is key. The cost can be extremely high – perhaps too restrictive for most small and even medium-sized businesses and start-ups.

Brightcove

brightcove.com
Video delivery at lightning speed

Brightcove is a video content management system that lets users create a custom experience for greater conversions and maximum ROI. Offering an established library of videos, on-demand publishing and live streaming, the suite also provides SEO-optimized portals with built-in lead capture tools and the ability to place ads within your videos using customer metrics, so that you can ensure each ad is highly targeted. Social media sharing combined with user-friendly templates make Brightcove a visually-pleasing, easy-to-use tool for sharing and distributing sales, training and marketing videos to audiences of all sizes.

Pros

No doubt about it, Brightcove is a major player, and it offers the lightning-fast servers and live-streaming capability you'd expect from a platform serving Fortune 10 companies. Streaming speed automatically adjusts depending on the device that's being used. The platform allows for a high degree of customization so you can make sure your brand shines through, and it also supports most major plugins with ease. Robust analytics and reporting capabilities round out the positives.

Cons

One of the biggest drawbacks to Brightcove is its price structure. Brightcove allows a set numbers of users and videos and a set amount of bandwidth for each plan tier – similar to many cell phone plans. Go over those limits, and your overage charges can mount up quickly. Overage costs vary depending on your tier. Determining your projected number of viewers and the bandwidth you'll need to accommodate your videos can be tricky. The good news: Brightcove has a team of specialists to help.

Constant Contact

constant-content.com/
Everything email marketers need

Constant Contact is an online marketing company that focuses on email campaigns. The goal is to build connections using personalized emails. The platform allows you to create a series of email responses based on triggers like birthdays, customer milestones and official holidays. The autoresponder sends the right message out for the right reason without any more time or effort from you.

This program is about managing both your list of email contacts and your use of email marketing. You create emails, set up the list and forget about it. The program will send the email out to every contact on that list based on a schedule. As you add new contacts, they begin receiving emails, too.

Extend your marketing beyond your inbox with Constant Contact. Create trackable coupons or online surveys, too. Everything is managed in this one platform

The tracking tool tells you who opens their messages, who clicks on links and who shares them with others via social media or by forwarding the email. All this is in real-time, so you see it as it happens and can act. The program also manages unsubscribes, bounces and inactive email addresses automatically.

Pros

Constant Contact works with a variety of email clients for contact lists like Gmail and Outlook. You can also create your own list via a spreadsheet. You can post your emails to social networks, too. The program suggests images and captions when you do. You are able to custom design your messages using CSS or XHTML. There are also premade templates you can choose from for your email layout. It takes about three steps to go from idea to send.

Cons

The program does not offer a cross-platform inbox preview, so you don't always know how the finished product will look.

ContentMX

contentmx.com

Content curation, creation and distribution from one simple interface

ContentMX was founded in 2008 to provide businesses and agencies with a reliable source of engaging, high-value, SEO-optimized original content that can be delivered via newsletters, blogs and social platforms to reach audiences in a way that's most likely to capture their attention. The platform allows you to develop and implement robust content strategies focused on the topics and the delivery format that are most appealing and relevant to your audience. ContentMX also offers a streamlined dashboard for content curation, allowing you to gather content from across the Web using sources you specify so you can easily collate, comment on and distribute it.

Pros
For smaller agencies and businesses that rely on newsletters for a major part of their marketing campaigns, ContentMX can be a great solution. The company founders have their roots in newsletter creation and distribution, so these features have been pretty much fully developed. It can also be a good choice for smaller agencies and businesses that want an integrated platform designed for one-click content curation intended to drive engagement and promote sharing.

Cons
ContentMX offers pretty basic functionality, making it a less comprehensive solution than a full-fledged CMS system. The dashboard, while streamlined, lacks some of the extras bigger companies may want, and workaround solutions can be time-consuming.

Cranberry

cranberry.com

Content redistributed to increase engagement

Cranberry is built on the principles of gist and brand recognition. Visitors to your site do not want to spend forever on a trail; they want to see the ending. Cranberry offers multiple content distribution settings to generate short-form content from long-form content. The site goes on to focus on native advertising, reinvigorating and emphasizing the style of your website, not an advertising agency's interpretation of your brand.

Pros

Cranberry has a dedicated pool of publishers, who work to get your message out. In marketing, the best message is usually the one that reaches your customers the fastest and most efficiently. Cranberry hosts a marketing radio station to help you learn more about content distribution, and the platform is built on four pricing models. Each model is available at lower rates than many national brands. The basic package is free and includes the ability to create an unlimited number of five-minute webinars. Gist Social, Cranberry and Gist PR (press release) include free registration, but Gist PR also includes a free marketing consultation. The cost of each package, paid annually, is broken down into publishing costs and promotion costs, making it easier to maintain transparency with your customers and clients.

Cons

Although Cranberry promotes plenty of publishers, it does not reveal their names. Unfortunately, you cannot control where and when your message is spread, with the exception of using five-minute webinars. The cost of Cranberry is another major drawback. Each subscription is limited to one company's campaigns, which makes it impractical for use in enterprise applications. However, agencies can request a custom, discounted rate when the agency plans to spend at least $15,000 monthly. Moreover, Cranberry does not offer a trial period.

Curata

curata.com
Feeding the content-hungry masses

Internet users are ravenous for content, and Curata provides the curation tool you need to keep feeding them promptly. Curata is a content curation platform that snoops out every corner of the Web around the clock for the most relevant, valuable content, which you can then deliver to your audience via multiple channels. These channels even include email and the customizable HTML5 site that comes with the software. Sharing third-party content helps to position you as an authority on what's going on in your industry and in related areas, especially since Curata lets you make annotations and add insights to all the content it gathers. Your comments keep your brand's voice alive while the incoming flow of content takes away the pain of manually scouring the Web for relevant posts.

Pros

Simplicity tops the list of Curata's benefits, as it streamlines virtually every step of the content curation process. The software's INSPIRE Discovery Engine finds the best content for you based on your preferences, industry and audience, allowing you to weed out the material you don't think measures up. Over time, Curata learns what kind of content you love and gets better at identifying trending topics. You also get a handy bookmarking tool to use while you surf the Web yourself, in case you come across something valuable. Your cache of impressive content can grow rather quickly.

If you're not a fan of the out-of-the-box site and blog Curata provides, you can integrate the software with your own content management system. Curata makes it simple to publish through WordPress and Joomla, although the included microsite is versatile, customizable and worth a look. Additional perks include an awesome search function, spot-on image recommendations to add flair to your content, a convenient mobile app and top-notch customer service.

Cons

Curata's analytics tool gets a big thumbs-down. The basic measurements feel elementary and generic. Although integrating Google Analytics with the microsite can solve the problem for your website, it can't enhance the insufficient email and social media reporting. The tool's limited screening abilities allow duplicate content to slip through the cracks, and the platform lacks a predictive content rating system based on traffic.

Eloqua

eloqua.com
Automation for complex minds

Modern marketers have a lot on their minds: nurturing leads, managing campaigns, targeting the right audience, and ensuring that quality content is delivered and published on time. Eloqua, a business-to-business content marketing platform, helps you get all those tasks out of your noisy mind and onto the screen, where you can streamline the entire marketing process. This automated platform specializes in content management and distribution, allowing you to better identify quality leads and share your content across outlets where those leads are most likely to tread. Real-time reporting lets you analyze your efforts for effectiveness, showcasing the distribution outlets that are failing and those that are bringing in the bucks.

Pros

The platform is packed with tools that help you with targeting, segmentation, campaign and lead management, and the nuances involved with social media and content marketing. Sales enablement features make it easy to align your sales and marketing efforts while customer lifecycle features let you personalize campaigns and build a loyal audience that keeps coming back.

And that's not all. The platform fully automates the entire content distribution processes, delivering an effective, efficient tool you can integrate into your customer relationship management platform. Another bonus is Eloqua's digital listening feature, which keeps track of page visits, email opens, contact form submissions, click-through rates and other statistics to measure the overall effectiveness of your efforts.

Cons

Complexity reigns as Eloqua's biggest downfall, as it takes weeks of training before most users are even marginally familiar with it. Some moan that even the simplest tasks seem to take forever due to a poor design that hampers usability, and trying to make sense of the reports is a challenge. Although integration is on Eloqua's list of features, it's been known not to play nicely with Salesforce, requiring a nearly full-time information technology team to make the two platforms work in tandem. One more complaint has to do with customer support, which was awesome when Eloqua was running the show but has notably deteriorated since Oracle took over.

Eventbrite
eventbrite.com
Self-service ticketing for getting the word out

Planning an event is only part of the journey. Eventbrite is the self-proclaimed largest self-service ticketing platform on the planet. You can create an event on Eventbrite in minutes, share the event with friends, business partners and acquaintances, and search for events to attend that peak your interest. When compared to the cost of payment processing centers, the cost of using Eventbrite is often much more affordable, and Eventbrite combines event management with event sales.

Pros
Eventbrite allows the sale of tickets on mobile and desktop devices, and real-time charts and data ensure you know exactly how much revenue has been brought in by your event. If you plan to host a free event, you do not have to pay for the use of Eventbrite. Eventbrite allows attendees to register individually or as a team, which is an excellent way to build and promote special discounts on paid events.

You can create a custom URL for your event, enable automatic reminders to attendees, create forum questions, and post different types of tickets for special guests, such as keynote speakers. Throughout the event management process, you can access all information about the event on a dashboard and set automated notifications for when attendees register or other changes occur.

Cons
Eventbrite is not a free service to paid events, and the cost per ticket sale can easily reach more than $10. Although you have the option of passing fees on to buyers, you cannot pass them on to buyers if you plan to accept PayPal. Payment processing fees are clearly identified on a buyer's invoice. If you plan to host a large event, it is difficult to create the event on your own. Creating large or multiple events

simultaneously requires a call to Eventbrite. Monies received for your events are not transferred to you until five business days after the event. In addition, you may need to wait longer for payment if you're location is difficult to reach by mail. Eventbrite does offer the option for advance event payouts, but the company charges a fee to access funds before the event is completed.

Facebook
facebook.com
Social media world leader

What started as a college networking site in 2004 has morphed into the world's most popular social networking arena, hands down. The latest statistics on the popular platform put the number of monthly users at more than 1.35 billion, with 65 percent of them checking Facebook every day. More than 1 billion users accessed the site through a mobile device in the first quarter of 2014 alone. Got an idea on how this can be useful yet?

In addition to setting up individual profiles, you're free to set up a company page that showcases what your business is all about. You can then post status updates on events and sales as well as provide links to your organization's own content or other online stuff you think your fans will enjoy. Companies have also used the platform to run contests, to invite their audiences to post photos or feedback, and to share their own photos, videos, infographics and anything else they think will rev up their followers and fans.

Pros
The platform's phenomenal reach weighs in as its top benefit. It easily outperforms all other social media networks for unique traffic referrals — more than four times higher than its closest competitor and more than three times higher than the rest of the networks combined. Facebook Ads offer another option for extending your reach even further. Facebook's versatility easily lends itself to all types of content and a variety of campaign options. It's also easy to use, and it offers a lot of support and training to help marketers reach a larger audience. And with its huge database of user activity,

targeting content to the right eyeballs is easier and more accurate than any other comparable platform.

Cons
As with other social media sites, it takes an ongoing commitment of time, energy and effort to really make Facebook work. Facebook also has a tendency to continuously change the algorithms and the rules, and if you don't follow them, you can't play. The company recently announced plans to cut down on content that it deems "overly self-promotional" and to stress quality, relevant and, more importantly, paid content. Thus, it may become trickier and more expensive to promote content in the future.

Google Plus
plus.google.com
Google-powered social media

When thinking about social media for content distribution, most think of Facebook. However, Google Plus is quickly becoming one of the more attractive options for businesses. The platform focuses on the best parts of social media, which include posts, images, videos and information. This helps keep visitors focused and engaged. Additionally, Google Plus automatically links to a user's Gmail account, and Google continues to develop and release new apps that will make the distribution process easier.

Pros
Google Plus uses your existing circle members to recommend others who may be interested in your products or services. Create polls easily on the site, and you do not have to worry about length limitations on your status updates. The Hangouts feature in Google Plus is nearly a reason to start using the platform in itself. You can set up a Google Voice phone number to connect to your customers through Voice over Internet Protocol (VoIP) through Hangouts directly, eliminating the cost of operating VoIP or a landline in your office. Create and host webinars and meetings within Google Plus, and invite others to view your work through collections you design.

Cons

Google Plus could be termed the "Facebook of Business." The platform has an extremely professional appearance, but it can seem dull and dry to new users. It lacks both the grandeur of Facebook and a built-in advertising feature. However, you can advertise if you create a new advertisement within each post. The value of Google Plus in content distribution is not realized until you have gained a sizable following. Another problem is the custom URL feature. Google Plus does not allow custom URLs until at least 10 people add you to their circles.

GoToWebinar

gotomeeting.com/webinar
Leader in videoconferencing

Give high-quality presentations and handle meetings on the fly with GoToWebinar's responsive web conferencing platform, an offshoot of its highly popular GoToMeeting product. GoToWebinar is designed to handle all your web-conferencing needs, from creating custom or template-based invitations and reminders, to creating follow-up emails with questionnaires. Interactive features let you create polls during your presentation for truly responsive and interactive engagement, including live Q&A, and the "record" feature lets you post your completed webinar on your site or via your social networks for expanded reach. In addition to capturing leads during the sign-up process, GoToWebinar provides plenty of analytics and reporting capabilities to help you fine-tune your marketing and analyze your deliverables, and mobile versions are available.

Pros

GoToWebinar offers real-time screen-sharing, making it easy to present PowerPoint screen captures and provide seamless live video streams. The annotation features allows you to circle words, phrases and images so you can add emphasis and keep viewers' attention, and you can also create and share handouts. Plus, GoToWebinar lets you rehearse rehearse your presentations ahead of time so they always look polished and professional. The platform also integrates with most CRM platforms, and you can customize the entire presentation with your logo and other branding features.

Cons

GoToWebinar requires participants to download the app to their own device, which can be off-putting to some users. Also, the platform uses Java, so both you and your meeting attendees will need to have the latest version installed in order to use the platform and all its features. You can't host your webinar directly from your own website, and there's no way to pay for a subscription-based webinar directly from the GoToWebinar platform. For most businesses using the platform purely for marketing purposes, however, the latter shouldn't really be a concern.

Infusionsoft

infusionsoft.com
Small business marketing marvel

Designed for small businesses of 25 employees or less, Infusionsoft aims to streamline the entire customer cycle. This sales and email platform includes a powerful suite of tools that help with customer relationship management, lead capture, marketing automation and e-commerce functionalities. The CRM capabilities let you easily organize all your customers and prospects.

Email and social marketing functions make it easy to stay in touch and automatically follow up with leads, while lead scoring gives you a heads-up when someone is ready to buy. Buying is also made easy with built-in e-commerce features that include on-the-spot sales updates. Top it off with return-on-investment tracking, automated marketing campaigns, and help optimizing Web forms and product descriptions, and you're looking at an all-in-one sales and marketing solution.

Pros

Infusionsoft goes far beyond your average automated email marketing platform. In addition to tracking each piece of content you distribute, the platform helps predict what readers will do after they open your initial email, allowing you to mold each email to trigger desired behaviors. Customer insights include a look at the different content media your buyers use on the way to purchasing your product, letting you focus on those that typically send a new customer your way.

When customers don't come your way, Infusionsoft helps you pinpoint problems that may exist with content and delivery, so you can hone in on specific issues rather than applying a blanket approach to weak sales. WordPress fans will also like that Infusionsoft is available in a compatible widget form to work with the content management system.

Cons

Although the monthly subscription fee of $200 may seem doable for small to medium-sized businesses, the one-time startup costs require a heavier investment of around $2,000. An equally heavy investment of time is required to undergo the extensive training needed to take advantage of the full functionality of the platform. The overall platform gets applause for being well-grounded, although some have complained of occasional tracking issues with leads.

Instagram

instagram.com
Instant visuals to the masses

Instagram had 10,000 downloads within hours of its 2010 launch, and it just kept growing from there. Although it was originally created as an easy way for people to share personal visual snippets of their lives, it was soon targeted by marketers that wanted a piece of the popularity. They're certainly getting it, with this tool distributing visual content to an enormous audience within seconds. More than 60 million Americans use the free smartphone app, which comes complete with photo editing options such as frames, filters and photo effects.

Pros

Facebook paid $1 billion for Instagram back in 2012, making it easy to combine Facebook and Instagram marketing. If your business has a

Facebook page, you can incorporate the InstaTab feature, which lets visitors to your Facebook page view and interact with your Instagram content. The 60 million American users constitute a huge audience on their own, but the audience is even bigger on a global scale. The app boasts more than 300 million active monthly users across the world. The bulk of those users are in the coveted 18-to29-year-old demographic. The laid-back vibe and interactive nature of the app is another bonus. Companies can engage with audiences in a more casual and humorous way than other channels allow. Engagement is encouraged with options for viewers to like, share or comment on your posted content.

Cons

The app was built for and remains an app most easily used on a smartphone, a drawback for folks used to managing and posting content from a computer. The tool also lacks any built-in analytics, which means you won't be privy to any campaign distribution statistics unless you're willing to download a potentially cumbersome third-party solution for help.

You'll also have a tough time getting Instagram viewers onto your website, or any other online location, as the app lacks any clickable links. Although the overall Instagram audience may be huge, targeting your desired audience segment can be difficult. Hashtags can help, but they can also be tricky to predict, plunging you into a lengthy trial-and-error process. You'll also spend a lot of time moderating comments if your posts end up targeted for criticism and spam.

LinkedIn

linkedin.com
Bountiful business networking

LinkedIn has become the go-to networking platform for businesses that really mean business. This free service was launched in 2003 and has since grown to more than 300 million registered members from 200 countries across the globe in just about every imaginable industry. As a member, you create a profile that resembles an online resume, highlighting your professional experience, education and even volunteer activities. You then are free to connect with individuals and join groups that share your professional interests. The site has built up quite a reputation as an employment hub, with 27 percent of its membership made up of recruiters looking to hire. Business-to-business marketers particularly adore the platform, with 94 percent of them using it to distribute valuable content.

Pros

One of the benefits of LinkedIn is the tools that allow content to be targeted to very specific niche audiences. Any member can now publish content, and LinkedIn kicks in to promote it algorithmically based on how many people read and like it. Premium membership options are available to expand the scope of services, and marketers can also choose paid promotion options known for being highly effective at targeting specific audiences. Not only has LinkedIn become a hub for recruiters, but it's also becoming well-known as a valuable resource for industry-specific news and information on products and services. It's an ideal place to research companies you may want to approach, provided they have filled out their profiles.

Cons

LinkedIn's high popularity contributes to its cons, especially since it opened the door for anyone to publish content. That means more and more content keeps coming down the pike vying for attention in a noisy, crowded space. Getting premium results increasingly means engaging in a pay-to-play game of spending to get the promotion required to gain attention. The connection process is somewhat cumbersome compared to other networking and social media sites, and the premium version that eliminates some of the site's annoyances is generally priced out of the range of many small businesses.

MailChimp

mailchimp.com
When you want to monkey around with email

MailChimp is about adding a little something, something to your email campaigns including a funny video or humorous message, but there is a little more to it. While enhancing your emails, this chimp is collecting data and taking names, too. With MailChimp, you use a drag and drop system to design campaigns that work. The collaboration tools like multi-user accounts and comments inside the editor make teaming up to create effective email campaigns easy to do.

Using MailChimp, you create targeted marketing campaigns, automated product follow-up and back-in-stock messages with just enough humor to grab their attention. This allows you to get the right email to the right person with ease. The built-in segmentation system allows for custom rules to create groups, as well. Use the reports to improve your email strategies for better email campaigns.

Pros

You get a lot in this little package. MailChimp has some great features that will improve not only your current email offering but help you design better campaigns down the road. The drag and drop editor makes putting images into an email fast and easy. The set-up takes just a few minutes and very little fuss. MailChimp costs less than some of the more sophisticated programs and even has a few free plans if you just want to try it out.

The advanced reporting system is available from anywhere, so you can monitor sales and website activity whether in the office or at home. The system also integrates with Google Analytics.

Cons

Humor is a double-edged sword, especially in business. MailChimp adds funny tidbits to your emails that not every business will want and some customers might find distracting. Although the company does offer some free plans, they do not come with analytics tools or an auto-responder. The reports from this program are not in real-time and the system is a little slow to refresh.

Marketo

marketo.com
Marketing automation gone wild

When it comes to marketing automation, there's not much Marketo doesn't do. The platform's powerful software toils ceaselessly behind the scenes to cover essential marketing tasks that many businesses struggle to find time to complete, including business-to-business marketing and lead management, email and campaign management, real-time personalization, and marketing management with budgets and calendars. The platform offers solutions for up-selling, cross-selling, and measuring and optimizing your return on investment and advertising spending. The site is also stocked with extensive blog posts, guides and other information that details marketing strategies, best practices and examples.

Pros
Marketo's huge lineup of features gets consistent applause, particularly the lead scoring and email marketing functions. Another notable feature is the ability to personalize content across multiple channels. You can create a message and let Marketo help you shape the content to best fit Twitter, Facebook or any other channel you choose.

The marketing management features are yet another plus. You can automatically generate budgets based on past information and then keep real-time tabs on your budget to see where it's going and whether your investment is performing up to par. The marketing calendar helps you track the content creation and publication processes.

Cons
Cost is one of the sticking points of this all-inclusive platform. Although Marketo offers four different pricing structures, the leanest option is still nearly $1,000 per month. Smaller businesses have scoffed at the cost, particularly when it comes with features geared toward larger enterprises that are not necessarily helpful on a smaller scale. The jury is also out on ease of use. A steep learning curve is involved to master the multiple functions, and even then, some users have found the system overly complex.

MyEmma

myemma.com
Email stuff that B2B marketers need

If you are a digital marketer looking for an email solution, MyEmma might be the right girl for the job. MyEmma is an email marketing platform designed with businesses in mind. It features tools that take your email campaigns from to start to finish efficiently and with eye-pleasing results.

Don't let the name fool you, Emma is actually a team of specialists that want to help you get results for your email efforts – ones that maximize success while minimizing effort. With this program, you gain access to custom template designs guaranteed to get their attention. Unlike other platforms, MyEmma provides specialists that review every campaign and offer tips to book opens and click rates before you start, so you get the most bang for your email buck. There is a spam checking tool that scans messages for keywords that might trigger a spam filter.

Emma also features a customizable database for handling bounces and opt-outs. You can connect lists created on Emma with spreadsheets and programs like Salesforce.com to connect everything for better marketing focus.

Pros

MyEmma stands out from other email marketing programs because it is really designed for B2B operations. Large-scale email systems like Constant Contact are a better choice for business to consumer connections, but this one is worthy of business to business. It has unlimited picture hosting, too.

Cons

It has a proactive support system, but no live chat. If you have a question or problem, you have to send a message and wait or stop and make a phone call. If you schedule an email to go out and then need to make a change, you have to cancel the campaign, make your fix and then set it up again.

Outbrain

outbrain.com
Nabbing new audiences for your content

Outbrain is a content discovery platform that puts your content in front of audiences you otherwise might not reach. This content suggestion tool uses widgets on popular websites to offer videos, blog posts and slide shows to readers who have demonstrated interest based on their prior surfing habits. Founded in 2006, Outbrain is the tool of choice for several high-profile brands, including CNN, Fast Company, Reuters and The Wall Street Journal. In November 2014, Outbrain signed a $100 million deal to become the exclusive recommended stories provider for sites owned by Time Inc., including the websites for People, Real Simple, Money and dozens of others.

Pros

Outbrain is the most well-established and well-known content discovery platform, and it puts your content in front of audiences from sites that are just as well-known. The focus can be any number of niche topics, such as entertainment, health or personal finance. The platform's commitment to quality includes a 2012 aggressive stance against spam content, a move that cost the company 25 percent of its revenue but earned respect from publishers and readers.

Analytics and geographic targeting are two beneficial features, as are customized widgets that publishers can use to ensure that your content fits naturally and unobtrusively into the content of their sites. Outbrain's suggestion modules allow you to put your content in front of new audiences without the use of invasive sponsored posts. You can also showcase a variety of content types, including videos, slide shows, quizzes, mobile content and blog posts.

Cons

While Outbrain did take a stand against spam in 2012, the platform had previously been accused of serving content with spammy or misleading headlines, so some publishers prone to holding grudges may continue to shun the site. Even if you embrace it, you can have a tough time gauging whether targeting a specific campaign will be effective due to the limited availability of data. In fact, Outbrain offers less complete data on its users than platforms such as Facebook do for sponsored posts. One more con is the price —a cost-per-click rate between 25 and 35 cents. This may make the platform too expensive for smaller content producers.

Pardot

pardot.com
Ready-to-go automation platform

If the potentially high up-front investment of time and resources is keeping your business far away from marketing automation platforms, you may find that Pardot is the answer. This software-as-a-service platform comes with the standard business-to-business marketing tools, including automated lead generation, lead scoring and nurturing, and database segmentation. But it doesn't come with the costly up-front investment for which other platforms are known. The company doesn't charge setup fees, and it also provides free training, making Pardot's no-contract, pay-as-you-go pricing structure an appealing choice for businesses with low risk tolerance.

Pros

Pardot treats you to a smattering of routine and out-of-the-box marketing campaigns designed to help you gain insight about current and prospective customer personas. Redirects link to images, content or static pages on your website, helping your team identify which elements attract more interest and motivate prospects to take action. Additional tools help you fine-tune frequency schedules with custom redirects, gather online profiles, and improve event management. More perks come from the ability to measure trackable behavior on social sites and third-party affiliates, replace drip campaigns with scheduled email to manage events, and add custom redirects to link blast email campaigns while identifying and measuring audience interest. Single-question poll and survey options help evaluate timing and frequency effectiveness, real-time alerts signal your sales team when prospects take action by clicking on a link, and a stellar support team backs it all up.

Cons

Even though Pardot is a Salesforce company, sync time between the two platforms is sluggish, with it sometimes taking hours to update edits made in Salesforce due to the slow communication process. The provided filters work well, but the limited report filtering and customization features don't offer enough options for diving deeply into the data. While the pay-as-you-go structure is a plus, you may be paying a lot if you go over the limit of the relatively low monthly maximum of 10,000 contacts. Additional fees may also pop up if you want to include key features that aren't included in the basic package, such as social profiling, Google AdWords integration, a dedicated IP address, and customizable user roles. Smaller businesses may find it tough to pay the $1,000 to $3,000 per month that a subscription requires.

Periscope

periscope.com
Live video through someone else's eyes

There are a lot of ways to track t numbers and count clicks, but how many chances to you get to actually see things as they happen through someone else's eyes? That is exactly what Periscope brings to the table. The Periscope app is guaranteed to be one of the coolest tools you try. It is a live video platform for iOS and Android that lets you stream things as they happen.

The app works in conjunction with Twitter to broadcast live video. When ready to stream, you tweet out a link and your followers click it to see what you see. You have the option to make the broadcast private, so only a select few can enjoy it or go public to let the world watch.You might be asking yourself how this fits into the content marketing puzzle. You have to think a little outside the box to put this tool to use for business. Imagine broadcasting live from a conference or trade show. How about broadcasting as customer tests a new product or service? The uses are only as limited as your imagination.

Pros

Periscope offers marketers a unique way to present content. Anyone can blog, but not every brand has live video streaming. The app works with Twitter, too, so it is easy to get the word out about a stream. Making it public means anyone can watch, so you open up your audience.

Cons

There are some legal issues with this app regarding copyright infringement like the live streaming of television shows or on-demand event. These have little to do with marketing campaigns, live broadcasts can be unpredictable. There is no time delay to protect you. Like any live broadcast, the stream may be unreliable or jumpy, too.

Pinterest

pinterest.com
Loads of alluring visuals

Crafters, photographers, artists and home decorators have discovered the joy of sharing their visuals through Pinterest, and content marketers have quickly followed suit. With more than 70 million users, this popular platform is a keen place to discover, collect, store and share amazing photos and other visuals. Set up an account and you are invited to create photo boards where you can pin content that falls into each board's category. You can invite other users to post on your boards, sharing their own stuff, and you can just as easily pull from other people's boards to highlight their content and give them credit for something cool.

Pros

Due to the highly alluring visuals peppered throughout the site, you're bound to have a least a little bit of fun every time you pay a visit to the platform. The service is free, and you're equally free to add any type of visual content you desire. This includes photos, graphics, infographics, charts, quotes and even a quick sketch of a new idea the CEO drew up on her morning coffee break. Each pin is hyperlinked to its source, whether it's pinned by you or by someone else, which means anything taken from your site gives Pinterest viewers a quick way to check out more of the same.

Pinterest generates more traffic than YouTube and Twitter, and people can pick which specific boards of yours they want to follow. This helps you fine-tune the content you place on each board to appeal to a very specific target audience. Pinterest buttons are easy to add to your Web pages, giving site visitors a super-easy way to share your content and its included link.

Cons

Companies saddled with crummy visuals or drunken photographers need not apply. The visual nature of the platform has generated loads of top-notch visual content, and you need professional images, graphics or videos if you wish to compete. You also need to pay acute attention to the hashtags and keywords you use in your limited text boxes to ensure optimal results. Eighty percent of Pinterest users are women, which is a huge plus for female-oriented products and services but a downer for companies targeting male audiences.

PR Newswire

prnewswire.com
Press release detonator

In the past 60 years, PR Newswire has grown into one of the largest network and business press release distribution sites. This paid content-distribution service helps businesses extend their digital reach — big-time. The site distributes press releases to more than 200,000 media points and more than 10,000 websites. Its user-friendly design comes with dynamic media and reach-tracking capabilities.

Pros

PR Newswire's massive distribution network is one of its major advantages. Its reach extends to thousands of media outlets, helping your press release gain traction and greatly enhancing the chances that it will be picked up by any number of journalists. That extensive reach is enhanced even further by PR Newswire's more than 675,000 pages indexed by Google, which translates to a potentially higher ranking and reach for your release itself. Improved media capabilities now allow users to embed images, videos, audio and other dynamic media right into their press releases. One more bonus is the release-tracking services that let you track your return on investment. You can compare how your coverage ranks to specific competitors, see where your news is being read, and discover which media outlets picked it up for repurposed publication.

Cons

Although the annual membership of $195 is not necessarily exorbitant, it may be enough of a deterrent for smaller businesses that don't generate a lot of newsworthy releases. Larger businesses that generate several releases per month are more likely to see a return on investment for the annual fee, but they still have to pay additional fees if they want their releases to contain graphics or logos.

They must also pay additional fees for any release that exceeds the maximum word count of 400. One more detriment is the press release availability, which is limited. Releases are removed from public view after one month and put into a password-protected database that is only visible to subscribers. That means your release has to hit hard and fast to matter, as it won't bring you any long-term search engine optimization benefits.

PRWeb

prweb.com
Fast and easy press releases

If press releases always sound like a good idea but a real pain in the rear, PRWeb may be able to help. This online press release distribution service not only sends your release out to search engines, news sites and its network of more than 30,000 journalists, but it gives you a ready-made template with which to do it. Take your newsworthy item to the keyboard and simply fill in the predesignated fields that outline the what, when, where, who, why and how designed to pull in traffic from interested parties.

Pros

Ease of use is the biggest draw for the service, mainly due to its ready-made template and helpful resources for newbies who may have no clue what a press release is all about. PRWeb lets you fill out a form and bingo— a press release is born. The wide distribution network includes search engines such as Google and Bing, social news sites such as Digg and Reddit, social networks such as Facebook and Twitter, and even your own RSS feeds. Not bad for a few minutes of work.

In addition to letting you choose which of the 250,000 different avenues down which to send your release, PRWeb will host your release on its domain, which receives an estimated 3 million unique views per month. Detailed analytics let you track the performance of your release across various channels, seeing how many times it's been shared, liked or otherwise acknowledged in cyberspace.

Cons

Fast and easy don't always mean high quality or worthwhile. Because anyone can generate a press release on PRWeb in minutes, the platform doesn't exactly enjoy an outstanding reputation as a valuable news source. This is underscored by the fact that PRWeb generally doesn't go out of its way to check the validity of the releases it sends out. Many of the sites on which PRWeb publishes its releases are sites devoted strictly to press releases — the kind of sites that make search engines gag. You may not necessarily want such sites associated with your business.

ReadyTalk

readytalk.com
Videoconferencing with no downloads required

ReadyTalk is a top-rated video-conferencing and webinar provider offering users a comprehensive set of tools to host events from just about anywhere in the world. Annotation tools, Q&A, chat and polling make every presentation an interactive experience for greater engagement. You can also appoint co-presenters and even grant access of your computer to attendees. Email invitations, automatic reminders and promotion on social networking helps boost attendance, and a suite of reporting tools provides an in-depth analysis for future marketing efforts. In addition to its video-sharing platform, ReadyTalk also supports audio conferencing, including an option that lets users host up to 150 guests on the fly for impromptu meetings and training sessions, without a need for invitations.

Pros
ReadyTalk supports audiences of up to 3,000, and unlike some of its competitors, attendees don't have to download a program in order to participate. It offers out-of-the-box integration with many top CRM platforms including Salesforce (for which it has a dedicated app) and Pardot. It also provides an open API that you can customize for your specific needs. Flexible pricing lets companies of all sizes use the power of presentations to promote their brands, and built-in tools let you easily promote your presentation on LinkedIn, Facebook and Twitter. Plus, you can share up to four video feeds at one time, making it a powerful tool for collaborative efforts.

Cons
For the best overall experience, users need to have the latest version of Flash installed. Considering some of the issues surrounding Flash – most notably with regard to vulnerability – this requirement may be problematic. ReadyTalk does offer a Java-based application for participants, but it's not as features-rich, and Flash is required to listen to recordings. If you want to offer full presentation via smartphones or tablets, you're out of luck; so far, Android users can only access the audio portions, although both the audio and visual portion of presentations can be viewed on an iPad. A single access code only permits up to 150 unique participants; for really big audiences, you'll need additional codes.

Shareaholic
shareaholic.com
Boost ROI with related content

Shareaholic may have started as a social sharing platform (hence the name), but since those early days, the platform has grown and expanded to include many other features. In fact, the platform is so widely used, the content it promotes garners more than 450 million unique views per month. As a Shareaholic user, you can promote your own work via related content links for greater visibility and engagement, luring site visitors to remain at your site longer. Built-in analytics help ensure you deliver the content each visitor is most interested in seeing, and affiliate linking and personalized native ads help you boost your site revenue even further.

Pros

As a long-term player, Shareaholic has an established and trusted reputation, and its website has evolved over time to incorporate plenty of easy-to-use, intuitive design elements, such as a streamlined dashboard and a simplified but powerful tool set. Shareaholic's tools help you understand what's driving your brand and create the content that's most appealing to your audience. Multiple templates are available in addition to its customization option, and thumbnails and text links are both supported. The platform's Recommendation Engine looks for content you can promote to help you build your site reputation while still providing you with full editorial control over what appears on your pages.

Cons

You must create a Shareaholic account, so if you're looking for a plugin that doesn't require you to complete a registration process, you'll need to look elsewhere. If you're only looking for a basic "related posts" plugin for WordPress, there are other, simpler options that might be more suitable. Although Shareaholic offers lots of customization options, it's not as full-featured as some of its competitors.

Silverpop

silverpop.com
Digital marketing ringmaster

Silverpop rocks for managing your entire digital marketing plan from a single spot. This integrative marketing tool provides a simple, intuitive user interface and works in conjunction with pretty much any other software out there. Designed for marketers who live for the hands-on approach to their campaigns, it provides a massive range of options for perking up your content performance. The main software offerings include the overall marketing platform, marketing automation, email marketing and an option called CoreMotives that brings automation and email together within the Microsoft Dynamics customer relationship management system. Silverpop's history dates back to the ancient era of 1999, making it a longstanding player in the content marketing arena.

Pros

Silverpop first started with a focus on email marketing, and email capabilities remain one of its strongest features. Sophisticated email marketing tactics range from simple blasts to complex multichannel campaigns, with the ability to track campaign performance and gain powerful behavioral insight. Help with retention and with transactional emails is available from the menu, along with automated targeted email campaigns that can be produced to suit any industry and scenario.

Other perks include high levels of flexibility to track and report on various marketing programs, a number of plug-and-play solutions, and all-around thorough reporting tools. Due to its ease of use, little to no information technology support is required to launch the platform; also, training videos and resources on the site provide education and industry advice.

Cons

Although Silverpop is a powerful program, it may have too many options that achieve the same result, which can be confusing to clients who are attempting to determine which tactics would work best for their needs. It can also be difficult to take full advantage of the myriad offerings due to the sheer number of options available. Customer service has been rated hit-or-miss, depending on who picks up the call. Occasional system glitches are par for the course, as is a slow-moving interface when dealing with a large amount of data. The system is better suited to small and medium-sized businesses with smaller amounts of data than to big data honchos.

SnapApp

Snapapp.com
Effective, thorough management tool

From creating interactive content to analytics capabilities, SnapApp is designed to boost traffic to your site and create an engagement-rich experience. Starting with templates, you can design all your content, and the built-in customer relationship management tools ensure all of your leads are carefully documented and vetted. This information is then combined with analytics capabilities to make following up on your contacts easier.

Pros

SnapApp is largely designed as a do-it-yourself tool. You only need to drag and drop content into place to create a branded experience for your visitors. Select from countless templates, libraries and design tools to ensure every aspect of your design process is flawless. You can vary your content type to meet practically any demand.

Once completed, SnapApp automatically detects what type of devices your visitors use and generates an optimized experience. At the same time, SnapApp reviews and monitors 30 data points within each item on your website to determine what is and is not working to benefit your company. SnapApp integrates seamlessly with major analytics providers, such as Google Analytics and HubSpot Marketing.

Cons

Since SnapApp is designed for those who want to control the entire digital experience, it can be difficult for the design-challenged to get started. Although the design is in drag-and-drop style, you still need to think about how it will appear when it automatically adjusts to fit different devices.

Unfortunately, SnapApp is among the more expensive content tools, and all subscriptions to SnapApp are billed annually. The starter package cost $1,650 monthly, which includes 10 pieces of content and access for two users to the SnapApp system. User access is capped at 10 users for professional subscriptions, but you can increase the number of users if you obtain a custom price quote.

Snapchat

snapchat.com
Free minicommercials for your brand

Social media represents one of the most innovative and cost-efficient forms of content marketing, and Snapchat is gaining notoriety for it quick, commercial-like applications. Snapchat allows you to create short video clips for distribution among your customers. You do not need to actively distribute the clips as your existing social media followers will help get your message out. Snapchat is an excellent tool for educating customers about your policies, products and vision for your company.

Pros

If you have used social media for your business previously, the pros of using Snapchat may seem redundant. It is free through and through. You are only limited by your imagination and your followers. Snapchat also boasts an impressive record in proven advertising, and the app is based on smartphones, not vice versa. In fact, Snapchat statistics claim up to 60 percent of the population uses the app daily, and you can create specific overlays to indicate your event, location or theme through Geofilters.

Cons

While social media is one of the fastest-growing forms of advertising, it is nothing compared to the advanced tools of the trade. Your existing SaaS analytics cannot track movement between your Snapchat videos, and your CRM software may experience difficulty in logging metrics from Snapchat directly. A mistaken upload could easily cause problems for your business, and it is extremely easy to become distracted within the app. If your product requires lengthy demonstrations, Snapchat may not be your best solution, and you may want to consider posting short introductions that redirect followers to your website.

Taboola

taboola.com
More eyes for your content

Getting your content in front of interested eyes can involve hours of painstaking strategies. Or you can go for a much quicker fix with help from Taboola. This content distribution platform places little ads featuring your content on its network of sites, giving those site viewers recommendations that align with their interests. Your site can return the favor (and potentially make some cash) by incorporating little ads featuring other sites' content. You know those "Content You May Like" boxes at the bottom of Web pages that send you to other sites with content similar to what you're reading? That's Taboola in action.

The network of sites using Taboola includes CNN Money, The Weather Channel and MailOnline. You can customize your Taboola-generated content through a feature called Taboola Choice, which further optimizes marketing campaigns and pay-per-click ads. Taboola works with mobile apps, and it is also associated with Taboola-X, which offers text-based advertising.

Pros

With 400 million unique visitors, Taboola is hailed as the world's most popular content discovery platform. One of its distinguishing features is the ability for viewers to provide feedback on content they do not like, so Taboola can provide more content that they will like. Another bonus is a detailed reporting interface where you can track content performance by site, placement, platform and country. Content publishers like the platform because it gives them a chance to monetize their sites with an option other than display ads. Content producers like it for its wide reach and notable network of sites that can showcase their content and generate more traffic.

Cons

Taboola uses widgets, which some have deemed annoying. Another criticism is the spammy content the program often recommends; it's not unusual to see Taboola-generated links to questionable sources on reputable sites. Similar content distribution platforms face the same type of spam complaints. The content picked up and shared by Taboola comes from the sites with the highest traffic, so you still need to keep your traffic-generating strategies in play if you really want to get noticed.

Tumblr
tumblr.com
Microblogging heaven

Got something quick, witty and engaging to say? Say it on Tumblr, a microblogging and social media platform that boasts 420 million users. Simply set up your site and rapidly post small doses of text, photos, videos, MP3 audio files and website links. Each type of content gets its own special category, making it supremely easy for users to find. Reposting other people's content comes with automatic attribution, giving your reach an even wider scope if people pick it up for their own pages. Tumblr works best with content that is easy to digest, such as funny images, hilarious video snippets and fast facts.

Pros
Tumblr comes with a highly active and share-happy social community. While traditional blogging platforms require you to build your readership from scratch, Tumblr gives you a ready-made audience hungry for entertaining content. Customization options let you stick with a Tumblr page template or create your own with a bit of design know-how. Images are the main draw, and they only require a few strategic keywords to make your post complete. The platform is hot for image-heavy companies, especially for Vogue, J.Crew and others in the fashion arena.

Cons
If you're looking to extend your reach beyond teens, you may need to look beyond Tumblr. The main demographic is the under-21 crew, which can be a boon or a bust, depending on what you're selling. You can also have a tough time targeting a specific audience or connecting with others, as the site is geared toward sharing content rather than building a legion of followers. Yahoo! paid $1.1 billion for Tumblr in 2013, and the organic feel that makes the site so endearing is already being challenged by Yahoo! Execs.

Twitter

twitter.com
Short, sweet, rapid blurbs

With more than 280 million active users, Twitter is the top spot for short and sweet tweets that don't exceed 140 characters. Individuals use the free social media platform for everything from making jokes to voicing complaints, and businesses can use it drive awareness, make connections and gain a slew of new customers and fans.

Twitter reports that 83 percent of small to medium-sized businesses would recommend the platform to other businesses, and using it is a breeze. You can employ it to provide real-time customer service, to communicate with your followers, to gain insights on your industry and customers, and to reach out to the influencers in your sphere. Twitter Ads let you extend your reach to even greater heights.

Pros

Twitter has a few cool tools to help you make the most of your tweets. One is the use of hashtags, which are basically keywords preceded by a number sign, such as "#hashtag." Clicking on a hashtag gives you a list of related hot topics, letting you review what's being said, so you can add valuable content to the discussion.

Sharing links is another biggie on Twitter, although you may want to use a free link-shortening tool, so you don't use up all 140 characters on an extensive URL. Other options include direct messages to your connections, marking tweets as favorites for acknowledgement or easy future access, replying to tweets, mentioning other users in a tweet, and retweeting other people's content.

Cons

With more than 340 million active tweets per day, your tweet can quickly disappear to the bottom of a mountainous heap. Tweeting multiple times a day can help, with some recommendations pegging the rate at one tweet per hour. Others suggest sending out the same tweet more than once, targeting different time zones and high-activity times for different audiences.

Photos and videos don't show up in your tweets, although you can include a link to a photo in your tweet to boost its allure. Statistics say that tweets with photo links attract twice the engagement as those that don't link to photos. The overall click-through rate of tweets is a low 1 to 3 percent, which is still higher than Facebook's average click-through rate of only .12 percent.

Uberflip

Uberflip.com
Flipbooks and much more to build your brand

Uberflip is a content management platform that lets you perform lots of tasks from a user-friendly dashboard which includes Smart Filters and automatic scheduling features so you can optimize your content for specific buyer personas. Initially used for creating flipbooks, Uberflip has evolved over the years to include much more functionality, emerging as a major player in content management systems. Content is managed via user "hubs" created on the Uberflip platform, and users have the ability to time distribution of content to "match" different stages of their sales funnel. Uberflip integrates with all the major social platforms as well as other content tools like Google Analytics and MailChimp.

Pros

A big "pro" for Uberflip is its ability to easily create interactive flipbooks for a far more user-friendly than traditional PDFs, and you can incorporate your own style, color and other features so each book reflects your brand (no coding skills required). Uberflip also lets you incorporate social engagement tools including YouTube videos for greater engagement or embed "clickable" CTAs and forms for data capture and better lead generation, then share your flipbooks via a custom URL. Plus, Uberbooks scores high marks from users for its customer support.

Cons

Subscribers to Uberflip's most basic entry level plan are restricted to a limited number of CTAs, and additional CTAs are only available by upgrading to the next levels. Currently, there is no way to set editing parameters across multiple folders to perform "bulk editing" tasks for brand consistency, which makes comprehensive editing somewhat tedious when broad changes need to be made. Finally, because the platform began as a tool for creating flipbooks, upgrades may not feel as seamless or intuitive as some systems which were designed for comprehensive management tasks from the ground up.

YouTube

youtube.com
Video jubilee

With a billion unique visitors every month, YouTube is easily the top platform for sharing all things video. From quick clips to vintage TV shows to makeup tips to music videos, your company's video content will be in very good company. Each uploaded video features HTML you can embed into Web pages, making it easy to share on social media and blogs. You can also opt for ads and paid subscriptions through the YouTube Partner Program to increase your distribution even further.

Pros

It's free to upload and host your videos on YouTube. The video and audio quality are both high, with a resolution of better than 1080p, which beats competing video platforms. The free service limits your videos to 15 minutes in length, but there's an option to upload longer videos with a Partner Program upgrade. With a free account, you can upload files up to 2 GB in size, while with a PP account, you can go as high as 20 GB. You can upload more than one video at once, and YouTube provides multiple encoding resolutions for viewers' convenience. Thanks to the multiple embedding and codec options, you can ensure that your YouTube video is compatible with a wide range of distribution channels.

Cons

To make the most of YouTube, companies are likely to need the paid Partner Program. The free service randomly chooses your thumbnail, for instance, whereas the option to select your own is only available through the PP. Customizing embedded videos can also be a hassle for anyone but tech geeks, and high traffic on the site often results in video lags. Private companies and public schools are known for blocking YouTube viewing capabilities, earning it the rank of the third-most blocked website in the world, which may limit your reach. YouTube is also plagued by zero adaptive bit-rate streaming, which causes substantial buffering slowdowns. Ads for your competitors may pop up on your banner ads or in the related video sections, although you can't advertise your own company on your own network.

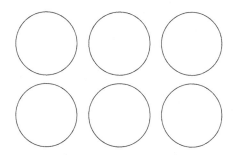

Content Performance

Tools for analytics, CRMs, heatmaps, and reporting

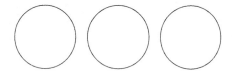

Adobe Analytics

adobe.com/marketing-cloud/web-analytics.html
Hardcore analytics bonanza

This powerful and popular content performance tool gives you a rundown on analytics you may not have even known existed. These analytics are aimed at helping you better understand a customer's thought process — or how customers go from passively searching your site to actively clicking on links — so you can guide that process to result in profitable actions. In short, Adobe Analytics provides tons of insightful data that can help you nab a sale. The realm of that insightful data includes advanced segmentation, predictive marketing, real-time Web analytics, marketing attribution, advanced data visualizations and mobile app analytics. As a whole, the Adobe Analytics tool set gives you detailed information on the strengths and weaknesses of your content's performance, so you can adjust it accordingly to ensure that it delivers.

Pros

The latest release of Adobe Analytics comes with a handful of new enhancements, all of which count as big pros for the tool. Improved mobile analytics — including in-app and personalized messaging — and a reimagined navigation system are two of the most notable. Others include improved flexibility, with the option of implementing customized solutions that resolve your specific challenges; return-on-investment enhancements, with the ability to quantify digital performance to better measure success; and easier integration with other Adobe products.

Reports have been enhanced with deeper details that let you run breakdowns, correlations and subcorrelations. One more perk is the multiple variables you can use to run more than 50 traffic, event and conversion variables. You can set variables to capture a variety of data points or to expire at a certain time — or stack them on top of each other, so you can analyze a series of events.

Cons

Like several other Adobe products, Adobe Analytics can be rather pricey. Cost is determined based on the size of your site and the type of package you choose, with AboutAnalytics citing the average at about $5,000 per month. Consistency, or lack thereof, is another con. User interfaces change across the Adobe platform, which results in a disjointed user experience. While the massive number of reporting options could count as a benefit for some, it may be overwhelming and confusing for others. Users have also reported that the response time for support and account management currently takes much longer than it used to.

Atomic Reach
atomicreach.com
Does everything but split the atom

Atomic Reach is a real-time optimization engine designed to improve the impact of your content. The goal of this product goes beyond just enhancing SEO or improving marketing campaigns. Atomic Reach works to make the writing at the heart of any content marketing scheme better. It does this by analyzing patterns and how the audience reacts to them.

How? The company uses an algorithm that predicts your content's success before you publish it. This allows brands to optimize writing style, quality, topic interest and relevance based on how well it is likely to do in the current market and with your target audience. The algorithm identifies key drivers by analyzing the behavior of your audience to see what makes them tick and how you can leverage it.

The technology reviews past interacts to see where content had an impact and what pieces fizzled. You use that information to make smart decisions about future topics and to curate your content to make use of the most effective pieces.

Pros
The information you get back with Atomic Reach is simple and easy to understand. The program looks at a post and rates it based on indicators like complexity, where it was shared and how often. There are no lines and lines of data to interpret or reports to filter. It is a simple and clear interface that anyone can use to publish the best content consistently.

Cons

Pricing is tricky for this product. It's based on the number of users and has some unfortunate limitations. If you buy the lowest priced package, you are limited to one user and one website. Even the second tier plan limits you to just one website. The most expensive plan has a two website limit.

Blitzmetrics

blitzmetrics.com
Content management broken down

Creating a successful marketing campaign requires time, and some campaigns can take months to get off the ground. Blitzmetrics is an all-in-one content platform for small businesses, enabling better content management with a focus on stress-free customer service. The team works with students to further drive costs down, and the entire process lasts six weeks from start to finish. Regardless of your experience and subscriptions, Blitzmetrics is among the most comprehensive platforms for complete content optimization, performance and management.

Pros

Blitzmetrics takes on the responsibility of setting up inexpensive marketing tools, such as Google AdWords, a branded Facebook page, and Google Analytics, for you. The site offers an extensive, 300-page guide on how the process works. Even if you choose to go with another content performance company, the insights from Blitzmetrics provide a path to success. Since students are the primary employees at Blitzmetrics, you have access to the latest technologies and innovations in content design and performance.

Cons

Blitzmetrics seems incomplete. While a free trial is mentioned throughout the site, it is not accessible unless offered via coupon code in an email from the company. Signing up for services through Blitzmetrics eliminates your control over the design and implementation process. Until access to your website is returned to you at the end of the six-week period, you must trust the company wholeheartedly with your information, which can be difficult for small-business owners. Blitzmetrics does not guarantee your satisfaction, and signing up for the company's services costs $1,500, making it out of reach for many.

Crazy Egg

crazyegg.com
Fun, insightful visitor tracking

Tracking the actions of your website visitors is a surefire way to ensure that your site is doing what you want, and Crazy Egg serves up a delicious way to do the tracking. As one of the most insightful content performance tools on the market, Crazy Egg functions quietly in the background to provide real-time and recorded data on how users access and maneuver within your site. You're able to monitor key factors that indicate how long a user stays on a given page and what the user views, making it easy to change your site to meet user, company or site-owner demands. The platform is easy enough for both newbies and pros to use, offering up a batch of valuable information that you can use to improve the overall performance of your site.

Pros

Heat maps are hot, and Crazy Egg has them. As users click through different links on a given site, the most commonly clicked areas on the heat map will show up as much brighter than other areas. This lets you see where users tend to flock, so you can determine the best design to enhance those sections of your site.

Crazy Egg's scroll map is another celebrated feature, allowing you to see how far down the site users scroll when visiting. With this tool, you can gauge whether important items need to be moved up on the page to a higher-activity location. The overlay feature lets you see the exact number of clicks on each link within a site with far more accuracy than other platforms do. Crazy Egg is one of the few content tools that will not confuse or combine the number of clicks for multiple links that are closely related.

Cons

The jury's still out on Crazy Egg's Confetti feature. Some say the feature provides way too much information that can end up being useless and confusing. Confetti shows you the exact places a user clicked, regardless of whether those were places the user was supposed to click. For instance, you may find users clicking on your phone number or static product images, hoping for a link that takes them somewhere.

Although Confetti provides a bevy of information about each click, including search engine optimization, user location, time clicked and other data, it fails to provide a full understanding of why the user clicked. Regardless, those who like the Confetti feature note that it provides insight on where they can add valuable links in areas where visitors already expect them.

Google Analytics

google.com/analytics
Free loads of data

Highly popular and absolutely free, Google Analytics rivals some of the higher-cost solutions as a valuable performance tracking tool. Once installed on your site, the tool provides a host of data that includes where visitors are coming from, what pages are prone to making them exit, and how they're interacting with specific content. You can easily keep an eye on traffic patterns for your most recent content to see if it's drawing a crowd. Tracking the performance of your content gives you the insight you need to keep visitors buzzing around by providing the type of content they continuously seek — while reworking the stuff that consistently turns them off.

Data can be easily exported in a number of formats for future or ongoing reference. Google Analytics is free for sites with up to 5 million page views per month. If your site is linked to a Google AdWords account, the analytics are free no matter how many pageviews your site gets. A premium version of Analytics is available at a cost for larger companies that need more in-depth features. A free version of Analytics is also now available for mobile app tracking.

Pros

The fact that Google Analytics puts massive amounts of information right at your fingertips — for free — is one of the tool's most-loved attributes. A prime example of this benefit can be found in the data related to advertising and campaign performance. In this area, you can enjoy advertising reports, live campaign measurement tools, mobile ad performance measurement utilities, and even search engine optimization reports. You can additionally import cost data into Google Analytics, allowing you to track your return on investment.

Cons

The lack of real-time statistics is a sore point for many users, especially as the digital world typically moves faster than the speed of light. A help center and user forum are the only forms of support for the tool, unless you're frustrated enough to hire a certified partner to get the support you need. The tedious practice of placing code on each page you want to monitor is another complaint, as is the feature that allows visitors to opt out of having Google Analytics track their online activities. Visitors with cookies and JavaScript disabled also cannot be tracked. Additionally, some users moan that Google Analytics doesn't offer suggestions for correcting poorly performing pages, a feature offered by other similar platforms.

Google Webmaster Tools

google.com/webmasters/tools
Website health check

Broken links. Malware infections. Mobile usability errors. There are plenty of things that can go wrong with your website that aren't apparent at a glance. Google Webmaster Tools is like the good doctor who periodically comes by to give your site a thorough checkup — absolutely free of charge. Unlike many real-life doctors, Google Webmaster Tools doesn't just tell you what's wrong; it also fills you in on what's right, such as popular keywords and links to your site. The tools gather the information by sending the Google bot to crawl your site, and you can also check how frequently those visits occur.

Google Webmaster Tools makes it easy to ensure that your website is in optimal health and performing up to par, a must if you want people to keep visiting it. All you need is a Google account and a website, and you can easily set it up by heading over to the online suite of tools found in the account pages' Google Webmaster Central area and adding your sites to the dashboard.

Pros

The free part ranks as one of the biggest perks, followed by the automated nature of the Google bot visits. In short, you don't have to do anything other than set up your sites and regularly check in on the results to fix any issues. Correcting flagged issues can greatly enhance the overall functioning of your site, and paying attention to inbound links, keywords and visits can help you optimize it.

Cons

This doctor will point out problems but won't provide any remedies. That part is up to you. Depending on the issue, this could be as easy as repairing a broken link or as challenging as revamping your entire site to address a long list of mobile usability errors. You won't find access to any experts for additional help, either. The tools only address issues found on Google, although they may give you a heads-up that the same type of problems may be cropping up with other search engines.

Hubspot Sales

hubspot.com/products/sales/sales-tools
Add contact insight to emails

Hubspot calls its Sales program a "sales acceleration product." Sales works in conjunction with the free customer relationship management, or CRM, system offered by Hubspot. With Hubspot Sales onboard, you gain insight into the activity of your customers, putting the CRM to work for you in real-time.

Sales puts you in control of one of your main communication tools. You know right away who opens your emails and who sends them directly to the trash bin. You see which emails convert into clicks, too. Hubspot

Sales runs in the background of the Chrome browser to provide live notifications when there is activity on the emails you mark for tracking. Sales comes in handy as you compose your emails, too. You have all the data within eyeshot as you write such as contact information, mutual connections and social media posts. The information is contained in a side window for easy viewing. After you compose your message using the details provided to you by Sales, tell the program when to send it. You have control over the time and date of transmission, too.

Pros

Hubspot Sales is available for no extra charge. All you need to do is add the extension to your Chrome browser to activate it. There is no additional configuration needed to make it work.

Con

The Sales stream connects automatically to all your Gmail accounts and combines them into one stream. That can get a little chaotic. You see business contact data right next to the notification telling you your mom read your email a few minutes ago. You can turn off the tracking per email, but the default is to track. You have to remember to turn it off.

KISSmetrics

kissmetrics.com
Streamlined strategy maker

You may know about a lot of things you and your team should be doing to really make your content marketing soar — things like truly understanding your customers, optimizing your marketing tactics, and outlining a solid strategy to increase conversions and keep customers happy. But just because you know about all this stuff doesn't mean you've found an easy way to collaborate with your team to do it — unless you've already discovered KISSmetrics.

This analytics platform brings key team members together to review and strategize, serving up a wide range of insights that can help you start that soaring. You'll see how customers interact with specific site elements, when engagement begins, and how to personalize Web experiences to increase sales. Comprehensive funnel reports, retention reports, A/B testing reports and cohort reports add to the mix, with additional reports and features available at the higher subscription levels.

Pros

KISSmetrics provides user-based timelines and tracks traffic sources in real time to see how they influence conversions. Most reports are easy to read, with realistic data assessments that offer versatility to meet customer needs. KISSmetrics allows properties to be attached to every customer, providing data on patterns of usage and campaign effectiveness as it relates to specific customers; you can even track users by channel. The funnel reports are known for being highly accurate, and they are especially useful for identifying holes and leaks. The KISSmetrics site is stocked with a bounty of informative resources that can enhance your efforts even further.

Cons

The same funnel report that can help identify leaks also gets a thumbs-down for having a steep learning curve. The system only allows tracking of funnels you have set up in the system; it doesn't help you find others of which you may be unaware. A few of the other capabilities, such as the user segmentation features, may be difficult to understand. Subscription plans start at $200 per month and extend up to $2,000 or more per month, price points that may be out of range for smaller businesses.

Mixpanel

mixpanel.com
Mix it up with user engagement data

Mixpanel offers app designers the chance to see how their customers use a product. It is a business analytics service that provides meaningful data that goes beyond pageviews and unique viewers. This program looks closer at user engagement, so you know what people are actually doing and can use that information to enhance your campaigns and improve your design.

The Mixpanel service provides funnels that give you insight into what customers are thinking. When someone tries an app, for example, how long do they use it? Are they getting confused along the way? At what point do they drop it because it doesn't work for them or they can't figure it out? Answering these questions helps you improve on your product based on how real actions. The funnel system is intuitive and flexible, so you can measure different flows as they occur to you. Through retention reports, you are able to visualize how your customers engage with your application, as well. Use this information to track and measure the effectiveness of the product to increase customer retention. With Mixpanel, you tie your company data to the users to see who they are and what they do in relation to your app.

Pros
Mixpanel can actually identify users and track their behavior over a specific time frame. That opens the door to more targeted marketing campaigns and data-driven decision making. With this system, you can track link clicks, JavaScript events and calculate retention funnels.

Cons
Although Mixpanel does a great job of tracking user behavior in minute detail, the user flow could be more flexible such as allowing you to set decision points for branching. The cost is a real consideration, too. Mixpanel provides a lot of data, but you pay for it.

Qualaroo
qualaroo.com
Picking your customers' brains

Wouldn't it be awesome if you could take a peek into your customers' brains to see what drives them to act? With Qualaroo, you essentially can. Formerly KISSInsights, Qualaroo is a software tool designed to find out what makes customers tick and, more importantly, what makes them convert. The tool gives you A/B testing and customer survey options, with the latter serving up real-time feedback from your customers on what they like and don't like — or whatever other information you want to receive based on the questions you ask. Customer feedback remains private, surveys can be targeted, and the software takes about two minutes to install. The layout has even been called stylish.

Pros

You can ask those stylishly laid-out questions anywhere along your sales funnel. You can even post an exit survey to get the skinny on why a customer did or didn't convert. Qualaroo can be customized to visually integrate into your website, complete with your brand's colors and logo. The easy installation involves the simple insertion of some JavaScript code. A free, 14-day trial lets you give the software a whirl before you invest in the monthly subscription fee, which starts at around $79 dollars for the lowest tier. Repeated applause seems to follow this tool wherever it's installed, with one user even calling it the "king of microsurveys."

Cons

The cost has been a turnoff for some smaller businesses, especially since one user noted the software was unable to accurately track response rates, giving statistics for impressions rather than unique views. Another caveat is the explosion of surveys and questions that frequently bombard the average Internet user. Marketers have been hot on the trail of obtaining feedback through everything from pop-up survey-taking requests to post-sale emails. Adding another layer of feedback-begging to the mix has the potential to repel those already annoyed by the constant slate of questions.

Raven Tools

raventools.com
Colossal marketing toolbox

Although reading multiple mounds of reports may not be considered fun, Raven Tools can at least make it easier and more enjoyable. Instead of hopscotching to different platforms to collect different report data, Raven lets you manage and report on all your Internet marketing through its single software app. More than 30 tools make up this efficient suite, including those focused on search engine optimization, social marketing, content marketing and pay-per-click advertising. SEO help comes from keyword suggestions for your own content as well as a play-by-play of your competitors' content usage. You can set up multiple content campaigns for multiple clients, with each campaign providing data on organic visibility, competitive analysis, link building, social media analytics, paid search advertising and keywords.

Pros

The sheer number of tools in this platform is one of its most amazing aspects, as is the sheer number of data sources you can harvest. Ravel Tools grabs data from a wide range of sources, including Moz, Google AdWords, OpenCalais, Alchemy and SEMrush. We all know that the more comprehensive the data, the more comprehensive your reporting will be, and Raven Tools gives you comprehensive with a capital C. Raven Tools also collaborates directly with Textbroker to provide content in the form of articles. This helps you continue to generate a steady stream of quality, optimized content you can stick in your library for future use.

Cons

Although you can manage paid search advertising with Raven Tools, you're limited to results within Google AdWords. You won't be able to manage ads on Facebook, YouTube or other social media platforms, nor is Raven compatible with Bing Ads. Those invested in PPC advertising on multiple platforms are thus pretty much out of luck. The dashboard provides a good start for content analysis, but it may be too elementary for those with advanced optimization needs. The overall platform is geared more toward startups and small to medium-sized businesses rather than larger enterprises. Syncing your data after the Raven Tools setup is a lengthy process. Also, for certain accounts, such as Twitter and inbound link widgets, you can access data only if you are actively connected to those accounts.

SimpleReach

simplereach.com
Content marketing crystal ball

Not sure where to place your content or native ads to get the biggest bang for your buck? SimpleReach can help. This software is designed to help companies, agencies and content publishers measure, distribute and retarget native ads or original editorial content across the channels that will produce the highest return on investment. The software measures various factors, such as engagement, reach and social activity, to qualify how content will perform on a variety of marketing channels such as Facebook, LinkedIn and Twitter.

The goal is to understand in advance how your content is likely to perform, giving each piece of content a grade based on the various factors to determine if it will be popular on any given channel. SimpleReach serves up both historical and real-time data to gain crisper insights and foresee the content performance future.

Pros

Using SimpleReach can help you determine where to focus your efforts and resources before you even spend that first marketing dollar. As one reviewer noted, similar programs are like a coach telling you what you did wrong after the game. SimpleReach is like one telling you how to play your best before the game even starts. Your helpful coach is not grasping at straws, either. The platform uses scientific measurements that increase its odds of getting it right.

Cons

SimpleReach requires a somewhat elaborate budget, with no free version available. The paid program is more complex than some smaller companies may require, and it's definitely beyond the needs of individual or niche bloggers. And no matter how insightful SimpleReach may be, you're still going to need to take the time to make sense of the metrics and devise your own strategic content marketing plan moving forward.

TrackMaven

trackmaven.com
Intelligent tracking

If you are a marketer looking for an easier way to create amazing content, look no further. TrackMaven monitors your content across all digital channels, so you have the data necessary to make smart choices. This product tracks social media, blogs, emails, paid ads, earned media, web traffic and SEO using sources like SEOmoz, Alexa, WharRunsWHere, MixRank and Compete.

TrackMaven is able to follow millions of content at once in real-time. It combines this information with a 3-year historical content store that covers tens of thousand of brands and influencers. With the right information, you know who your competitors are and learn for the industry influencers. Find out what brands are making it work and what they do right, too. With this metric system, you can use competitive benchmarking to track what your products and brands to compare to others. Use that information to focus your channels, topics and formats, so they work in your favor.

Pros

TrackMaven offers an intelligent report system that allows you control over how data is analyzed and filtering. It provides both strategic data and personal alerts with effective features like a universal feed, custom visualization and real-time benchmarking.

The information that you get from this system allows you to make immediate changes to improve a campaign, whether you are just beginning it or somewhere in the middle. The customer service team at TrackMaven gets high marks for providing effective support, as well.

Cons

For the most part, users are very positive about this technology. The one downside seems to be the complex subscription system. Pricing is based on a number of factors such as how many users you track, competitors and types of data.

Webtrends

webtrends.com
Make your marketing trendy with the right data

Webtrends provides businesses with data-driven solutions designed to improve their marketing efforts. This company offers a diverse portfolio of services that organizations can use to enhance their online presence and target their digital campaigns. It is up to you to pick the option that best meets your needs. Social analytics help you expand your networking capacity, for example, or use the mobile data to fine tune local ads.

The Webtrends products offer real-time data that spans channels to provide solutions that are both individualized and actionable. The company uses top-notch technology and their team of experts to create targeted options based on social media activity, geography, age and purchase history. They then export the data to you for use in creating effective and efficient marketing campaigns. You cluster the services together that you need such as segmentation, analytics and testing, so you only pay for what you can use.

Pros
The Webtrends products are available as software or on demand through software as a service (SaaS) models. The package offered is sophisticated, yet user-friendly, so anyone can master its basic use. The ala carte business model allows you to pick and choose what you want without having to work around segments that you will never need.

You can go online for support and training, as well. The training section offers how-to videos that you can use to train one person or a group. Webtrends also offers courses designed for technical professionals and network administrators who must configure their products. They also offer certification courses and an administrator exam.

Cons
The software is complex enough that it may require extensive training for IT professionals to customize reports. The classes offered by Webtrends for administrators are not free, either. The software is a little pricey compared to similar packages.

Wistia

Wistia.com
Get your video on

Wistia lets you take your marketing to the next level – and that means video. This Internet video hosting service does more than just play the video, too. It offers analytics and external stats for better monitoring that include heat maps and metrics for skipped videos and restarts. Started in 2006 by Brown University graduates Chris Savage and Brendan Schwartz, today Wistia is an international service with "...the best marketing tools in the (known) universe."

While the company slogan might go a little too far, there is plenty to love about this product. Wistia puts you in complete control of your videos by restricting where they are played and how they look on social media sites. You get a better understanding of how your video marketing campaigns are working and whether they are leading to conversions.

Connect Wistia to your favorite email client and capture leads and add them to your email list automatically. By using JSON-LD for videos, Wistia ensures that your videos rank for pages, too. The features available with Wistia assist with the generation of embed codes, customization of the player at the back end and the integration of closed captioning and transcripts. Before you know it, passive audiences become interactive.

Pros

Videos uploaded to Wistia have multiple resolutions available. From there, you can choose what controls you want in place and whether to add social media buttons for sharing. The viewer-to-lead conversion option means better email marketing campaigns. Wistia also includes a call to action choice that guides viewers at the end of the video.

Cons

The free plan ends after three videos. Wistia is not searchable like YouTube, either. Most sites cater to YouTube, as well, so integration can be tricky, but is usually possible

Woopra

woopra.com
Visual, in-depth analytics

If you're into snazzy visuals to help you understand customer behavior, Woopra may top your list of analytic platforms to use. The platform's triad of power comes from three main features. Customer profiles give you a full-scope, in-depth profile of every single user, starting even before people provide any information and are still anonymous visitors to your site. Real-time analytics let you set up customizable options for segmentation, retention, funnels and other fun facts. AppConnect allows you to automatically bring in and centralize data from your other tools, such as WordPress, email marketing, or help desks, as well as automate data-driven actions, such as displaying personalized content or finely targeted email campaigns -- all without a single line of code. And then, there are the visually oriented metrics, making everything easy to read at a glance. One more plus is the seamless way Woopra can be incorporated into your own site, providing a solution that looks like it was custom-made just for you.

Pros

Woopra easily integrates into a host of other tools you may already be using, such as MailChimp, MySQL and WordPress, giving you access to all your data from a single location. The pricing structure is flexible, letting you pick and choose your plan based on how many actions you want to track per month. The small business options range from about $80 per month to track up to 400,000 actions to about $1,200 per month for tracking up to 10 million actions.

Small business plans come with 10 seats — in other words, reporting access for 10 team members; an enterprise edition is available by contacting the sales team. Real-time results are another plus, especially since Woopra stores data in funnels that can make it easier to make decisions over time.

Cons

Although Woopra is big on integration, some say it's not big enough. Some users would like to see more integration options with additional third-party tools. Google Analytics contains more options, including its own ever-popular AdSense and AdWords. Other Woopra annoyances include the inability to adjust smaller details on the reports, such as column width, and limited customization and layout options in the updated Woopra dashboard. Longtime users have complained that each updated version of Woopra seems to include more and more tools that don't do anything other than add unwanted clutter to the dashboard.

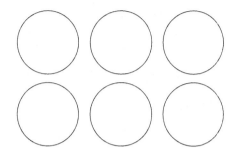

Content Management

Tools for CMS, content management,
and asset management

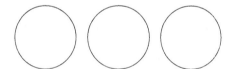

Adobe Business Catalyst

businesscatalyst.com
Business websites for serious business

Geared toward Web designers, Adobe Business Catalyst serves as a one-stop shop for creating a comprehensive business website. The content management system includes options for analytics, blogging, e-commerce, email marketing and a host of forms you may need to create and maintain a site. Additional features include Web hosting, email, cloud backup and the ability to integrate with payment gateways and social media. Yeah, it does a lot, serving as a more advanced solution than the popular but somewhat elementary WordPress and as an easier alternative to more complex platforms such as Drupal.

Pros

Adobe has a solid reputation for creating high-performing software, and Business Catalyst measures up. The all-in-one setup makes it easy for programmers to set up a completely integrated site without a lot of added plug-ins and services. The e-commerce abilities are top-notch, giving customers easy navigation. The cloud-based backup provides maximum data protection. The system is also hailed for its nifty newsletter component and high-quality customer relationship software.

Cons

As noted in the first line of the summary, the software is geared toward Web designers. That means anyone with limited knowledge of website workings may find Adobe Business Catalyst to be a poor fit. Actually, anyone without technical know-how on back-end issues, such as coding, will find it difficult to use. This holds especially true for small businesses that wish to emphasize blogging, as the blogging component is one of the platform's least user-friendly features.

While the cloud-based backup is tops for security, it's not tops if you're looking for full control over all your content. The system will not allow you total access to all parts of your backup, a quirk that leaves some users frazzled.

Adobe Experience Manager

adobe.com/marketing-cloud/enterprise-content-management.html
Full-featured CMS powerhouse

Adobe Experience Manager is a content management system that's part of the brand's marketing cloud solution, allowing users to create and manage their marketing assets, including websites, apps and forms. With the Adobe name behind it, it's no surprise the Experience Manager is used by some of the world's leading brands to drive marketing content on websites and social platforms, and the latest version makes many of these powerful features more readily available to smaller businesses as well. Adobe draws from its vast experience in the digital space to provide the tools that enable brands to create deeply-engaging customer experiences at every stage of the sales process, earning it top marks from Forrester Research.

Pros

Adobe has a long and established presence in creating platforms that are user friendly, and Experience Manager is no exception. It provides an interface that's designed for ease of use. The selection of templates and other components results supports flexible design, allowing users to change the hierarchy of the content they offer both before and after publishing. In addition to its own set of reporting tools, Experience Manager is designed to integrate seamlessly with other leading tools and platforms both from Adobe and from other companies, and the platform's mix of default and customizable features enable each user to create an experience that's truly reflective of their brand.

Cons

Experience Manager can be a good solution for large enterprise applications, but for smaller companies, many of its features probably won't see much use. It's quite expensive, making it prohibitive for businesses with smaller budgets. It's also not an ideal choice for e-commerce applications. Adobe recently added several new updates, some of which are a little finicky; however, additional planned updates and patches will likely smooth out these bumps.

Blogger

blogger.com
Really, really easy blogging

Have you always wanted to start a blog but are not sure where to begin? Begin with Blogger, and you can have a free blog up and running in minutes. OK, maybe it'll take a little longer than that, since you still need to produce some content to make your blog active, but this free, Google-owned blogging tool makes creating and maintaining a blog as easy as breathing. Simply sign in with your Google account and then pick a blog name, Blogger template and colors, or further customize with your own uploaded images. Blogs are viewable on Blogspot.com and are linked to your Google+ account. You also have the option of uploading your blog content to your own website, although the template will not follow. You can, however, use the tool as the basis of an entire website thanks to the variety of compatible themes and widgets.

Pros

The platform is refreshingly simple. It's easy to navigate and uses generic terms even first-time computer users can understand. Because Blogger has been owned by Google since 2003, Google has had plenty of time and a wide scope of resources to ensure that the tool is stable and secure. You can easily post from any mobile device and have the option of integrating Google AdSense, which opens the door for monetizing efforts. Blogger also comes with its own content analytics, letting you see the number of pageviews and overall views your blog amasses over time.

Cons

Blogger has been around for more than a decade, and the dated look of many of the style and template choices proves it. Lack of support on the Blogger platform is another downfall, as is the inability to change the back-end code to customize your blog to your exact needs. While you can set up your own personalized blog name, your blog URL ends up as yourname.blogspot.com, which doesn't give a professional impression.

Buffer

buffer.com
One-click, timed content publication manager

Buffer is a powerful CMS tool that uses a queue system to automatically distribute your content at predetermined time intervals, ensuring your target audience gets the right content at the right time for more clicks, higher traffic and increased conversions. Content is distributed at the best times during the week and during the day to attract more eyes, so your content is more visible and garners more shares and likes. Plus, Buffer offers a suite of powerful publishing tools to make it easy to distribute content on multiple social platforms with a single click. Photos and videos are also supported, and the new Pablo tool lets you create custom images and share them via your social accounts. In addition to the browser version of Buffer, Android and iOS versions provide on-the-go access.

Pros

Buffer integrates well with all the major social networks and content management systems so you can manage content using one streamlined, user-friendly interface. Evolving analytics provide plenty of data you can use to optimize content and delivery, including tools that analyze past performance to help determine the best publishing strategy. Buffer is also known for its fast and helpful customer support team.

Cons

One of the biggest drawbacks to Buffer is that you cannot republish evergreen content automatically; instead, you'll need to re-enter it into your queue so it can be rescheduled and delivered. Buffer also is no substitute for a complete SEO management suite with monitoring and comprehensive analytics; rather, it's a tool which works well in conjunction with a bigger CMS to enhance content management.

Canto

canto.com
Fully integrated digital asset management

Canto's award-winning Cumulus digital asset management platform relies on metadata analysis to help businesses of all sizes collect, create, organize, edit, distribute and repurpose multimedia content with an easy-to-use interface that can be deployed on-site or in the cloud. Fully scalable and deployable on local, regional and multinational bases, Canto's DAM platform is designed to integrate seamlessly with other CRM systems, including leading CMS, ERP, PIM and e-commerce platforms via a powerful RESTful API. Cumulus portals let you share large files while promoting and protecting your brand, controlling digital licensing rights and limiting usage with read-only and download-only options. Workflow automation features let you assign tasks and manage processes for hassle-free creation and distribution.

Pros

Cumulus offers an amazing degree of customization, which means if you invest the time in learning the system, you can carry out just about any vision for your digital assets. Canto's responsive support team helps you when you can't find the solutions yourself. The InDesign Client and Adobe Drive Adapter let you access and manage content from within a wide range of Adobe applications, including InDesign, Illustrator and Photoshop, with Cumulus tracking all changes as they're made. Version control features let you track changes – even tiny ones – and roll back content to previous versions, all with the touch of a button.

Cons

Canto's Cumulus platform is big – so big, it can take a considerable investment of time to identify, learn and implement its most useful features. As with any large and full-featured platform, there is a learning curve.

Content Launch

contentlaunch.com
Content creation, marketing, consulting

Building a backbone of quality content doesn't need to be a pain in the neck if you opt for help from Content Launch. This content-centric, subscription-based company provides a wide variety of services, including content creation and content strategy consultation. Pay a monthly subscription starting at just $100 per month for access to their content marketing platform which allows you to plan, create, collaborate and score your content. (Content Launch also offers a freemium version)

Content Launch also offers customized, high quality content from the platform's pool of writers, with a flat fee based on the type of content you need, starting at just $70 for a high quality blog post. Or hire the Content Launch team to provide a comprehensive content strategy designed specifically for your business. Strategy consulting costs start at $2,000.

Pros

A wide variety of content choices and experienced writers are some of the pluses Content Launch offers. Content choices range from blog posts to emails to white papers to e-books. The platform boasts 300 writers experienced in both business-to-consumer and business-to-business content creation, with expertise in more than 70 industries. You can pick and choose the services you want, which means you can purchase content without a platform subscription or purchase a platform subscription without purchasing any content. Consulting services can also be purchased separately.

Cons

Although building content with Content Launch may not be a pain in the neck, it can be a pain in the wallet. The platform's products and services are on the costly end of the scale and are likely priced out of the ballpark for smaller businesses. The cost of integrating the platform does not include the cost of creating any content. Content revisions are also limited to two, unless you want to pay extra for additional tweaks.

Contentful

contentful.com
CMS with a mobile-ready focus

Contentful uses the cloud to enable users to manage their content across a variety of platforms, including social networks and mobile platforms, providing seamless integration and interactive content management with a responsive editing interface. Unlike competing products that have been modified over the years to address the rise of mobile platforms, Contentful was developed with mobile responsiveness at its core, featuring an API designed to address the unique requirements of mobile delivery. The platform uses a back-end interface to allow real-time collaboration on content creation and editing, which is then published to the Contentful API and finally distributed according to your own preferences. Both "freemium" and paid versions are available.

Pros

Contentful is platform agnostic, meaning developers aren't constrained by the templates and other restrictions unique to software-based CMS platforms like WordPress, allowing unprecedented freedom in creating and distributing all types of content and a near-limitless number of templates. Content can be previewed on different devices prior to publishing so there are no unpleasant surprises. Instead of storing content in pages that can slow down delivery and responsiveness, Contentful uses "entries" which allow for far greater flexibility and speed. Plus, Contentful uses Amazon Web Services for lightning-fast delivery using multiple redundancies and extensive caching, so even if a problem does arise with distribution, content can still be delivered from the cache. An active community of users and Amazon's customer-centric model ensure troubleshooting is fast and straightforward.

Cons

The primary downside to Contentful is its new delivery system, which seasoned CMS users may find difficult to navigate at first. A wealth of templating and design options may also feel overwhelming, and there is a definite learning curve.

Cvent

Cvent.com
Leading event management and registration platform

Hosting a conference, trade show, seminar or webinar can be one of the best ways to attractive visitors to your business. Unfortunately, getting the word out about your event and managing the event from start to finish are extremely difficult. However, Cvent offers complete event management, which includes online event registration, venue reviews and sourcing, and the ability to manage your event through mobile apps. Cvent has garnered the attention of over 166,000 users, who manage and measure the success of their events through surveys, feedback requests and more.

Pros

When it comes to event management, Cvent leaves you with nothing to worry about. You can decide what needs to be implemented, what metrics will be tracked, such as budgeting and speaker addresses, and review the success of your event after it is over. Cvent goes on to create multiple apps for you and your event. For example, you can create an app to allow attendees to manage their plans and networking responsibilities and capabilities at your event with your brand in place.

Advanced analytics within Cvent help you determine which attendees expressed the most positive views of your events, what events were most participated in, such as individual workshops or sessions, and how your event stacks up against similar events online and through social media. In other words, Cvent strengthens the argument for attending your event and conducting business with your company without the drawbacks of involving a third-party provider.

Cons

The problems with Cvent are minimal. The customizable features Cvent can make designing the apps and respective websites difficult. Workflow management is not necessarily linear, and you may need to shift between different parts of your event in order to effectively manage it. Additionally, Cvent claims to support integration through WebEx, but WebEx integration suffers if you need to change or cancel the original plans of your event.

Double Dutch

doubledutch.me
App-based event distribution and management

Double Dutch is an event marketing marvel. The site provides advice on event management and creation for corporate level to small-business owners. Major companies, such as LinkedIn, Forbes, Time and Humana, have used Double Dutch to market their events. The Double Dutch app combines engagement and event performance by engaging confirmed and prospective attendees and providing finite analytics for the duration of your event.

Pros

Double Dutch is entirely customizable, allowing you, the organizer, to create an event setting within the app with full branding and custom layouts. Double Dutch also includes promotion tools through connecting attendees with other attendees across social media and other networking platforms. Double Dutch goes on to enable users to receive welcome emails, which are sent automatically or manually at the organizer's request, and you can track installs of the app.

Double Dutch also includes live question and answer forums, surveys and live polls. In the polling feature, you can gain real-time insight into how attendees feel about the capabilities of organizers and presenters prior, during and after your event.

Cons

The cost of event distribution and management through Double Dutch varies heavily and depends on what sales you have and what sponsorships you undertake. Since the app can be used on a global scale, event management can be made difficult in currency translation and due to cultural barriers. For example, a prospective attendee may post comments in the form in a different language. Additionally, the level of customer support available is determined by what level of package is purchased.

Drupal

drupal.org
Mind-blowing content management system

Drupal is an advanced content management system with the power to blow your mind. The mind-blowing comes not only from the high levels of customization and creativity the platform can provide but also from its complexity and sophistication. The free, open-source platform can be used to create everything from the smallest blog to the largest e-commerce site, tailored to fit any and all needs. While designers appreciate Drupal for its wide-open range of creativity, the platform also offers ready-made modules and themes to give you a head start on your site. The platform originally hit cyberspace back in 1999, so it has had plenty of time to establish a solid reputation as well as a supportive online community.

Pros

Drupal comes armed with tons of functionality, including the prebuilt CKEditor, which is a WYSIWYG text editor that contains buttons for automatic formatting and table and image insertion. Site administrators can choose between rich text and plain text editing and between filtered and full HTML support. Blocks are Drupal's way of managing sections of text on a Web page and locking those sections into particular spots. When you install Drupal, you get three main pieces, each of which can be customized with its own theme and tailored to perform specific functions.

Other perks include an integrated comment system and advanced management of menus, polls, users, graphics and a wide variety of content types. The support of the well-established online community is bolstered by a chat option, discussion board, mailing list and on-site documentation.

Cons

Although Drupal far surpasses WordPress and Joomla in both functionality and complexity, it is far from user-friendly, requiring advanced know-how to install and modify. Additionally, Drupal's back end is less intuitive than that of some other content management systems. Each menu item opens in a subwindow in front of the site preview window, which can make things difficult to see and can complicate navigation for new administrators. It's also easy to accidentally close the subwindow. Most Drupal administrators will want to develop their websites on a local host before installing them on the live server. Site administrators must familiarize themselves with Drupal's back-end layout, various menus and tabs, and the blocks function before creating content.

Joomla

joomla.org
Heavy content CMS

More advanced than WordPress but less robust than Drupal, Joomla falls in the middle of the content management system lineup when it comes to complexity. It ranks as the seventh most popular CMS in the world, and it's particularly popular with programmers, who use the open-source platform to build a wide variety of site types. The system's high degree of flexibility allows you to build anything from a simple blogging site to a more sophisticated e-commerce site. It's especially hearty for multimedia sites or those containing tons of content.

Although it doesn't have as many available plug-ins as WordPress, you may not need as many. Joomla refers to plug-ins as "extensions," and it does have thousands of them available right from the homepage. It also comes equipped with more functionalities than WordPress from the get-go, boasting included features that would require a handful of WordPress plugins to achieve. The platform is free to use and is available through a download.

Pros

Easy installation starts the list of benefits, with the process taking all of about 10 minutes. An extensive amount of support is available on the site, with options that include tutorials, programmer tools and a discussion board stocked with a large and supportive user base. Frequent updates continuously add new features while fixing existing bugs and security concerns. Benchmark tests have suggested that Joomla performs faster than WordPress.

Cons

Those same benchmark tests that ranked Joomla as faster than WordPress deemed it slower than Drupal. Limited templates and modules may be irksome for more advanced users, and some of the extensions and modules come with a fee. Compatibility issues can also crop up between extensions, requiring extensive code adjustments to correct. Due to being more complex than WordPress, Joomla has been known to send newbies fleeing in terror. Joomla is definitely geared toward those with solid CMS experience.

LiveJournal

livejournal.com
Connections through journaling

We've all kept a journal at least once in our lives — our third-grade teachers generally made sure of it. LiveJournal gives you the opportunity to dust off the concept of journaling and use it to make connections, engage your audience, and share company or personal insights on its unique social media site. Instead of quick status updates or 140-character tweets, LiveJournal lets you share journal entries, which are equivalent to blog posts. Each journal entry has its own page, while a separate table of contents page lists all your journal entries. Set up a profile, add a photo, pick your interests, and you're ready to roll. Sharing and commenting options make it easy to interact with fellow journalists.

Pros

With a young demographic of 10 million users, LiveJournal has the potential to serve as one of those hidden gems you're always hoping to stumble across — a fresh, new audience that helps you expand your company's reach. Those in the user base tend to be active on the platform, eager to engage with content that meets their interests. Free accounts offer limited features that can be substantial enough for basic users, and creating a new journal entry is a snap.

Cons

Due to the limited amount of guidance available on the platform, hunting and pecking your way through the features may be a way of life as you get started in your journaling experience. The more advanced features, such as analytics, polls and domain forwarding, are only available with the paid version of LiveJournal. Every journal is also peppered with ads, with fewer ads on the paid version.

Customization is possible, although it requires some HTML knowledge. The editing tools are rather limited and clunky, making formatting a challenge. The overall appearance is also outdated, and early users complained that the interface seemed to do a good job of hiding essential features. Because there is such a focus on community, this is not a place where you'll get much traction from pulling a post-and-run. You'll instead need to make the necessary investment of time and energy to make meaningful connections that could possibly result in a return on investment.

NewsCred

newscred.com
Targeted delivery for all types of content

NewsCred initially began as a consumer news site, gathering stories from across the web and from other sources and presenting them in one convenient and credible site. Over time, the business model evolved to include content marketing, focusing primarily on sourcing content for other companies – including big names like Toyota and Pepsi.

More recently, NewsCred raised nearly $100 million in capital to expand its platform and its functionality, with new features being rolled out regularly. The platform has introduced new, cutting-edge technology to improve performance and provide plenty of support for its new features, helping companies of all sizes find and distribute a variety of content targeted at their audience's needs.

Pros
NewsCred is easy to use, with a simple interface and useful – if relatively basic – functions. However, the recent influx of cash is enabling the product to grow and evolve to include plenty of tools for broader content management tasks, with plans to include options

like management of TV advertising within the same platform. The company prides itself on efficient, responsive customer service.

Cons
In its earlier form, NewsCred was hindered by its lack of functionality as it worked to carve out its place in the broader content marketing landscape. New features have been (and are being) introduced, which means there may be some degree of frustration in learning new skills to take full advantage of the platform. It also makes difficult to determine whether NewsCred will meet your business' current needs and be able to grow as your business does.

Percussion
percussion.com
Browser-based CMS focused on ease of use

Percussion is a user-friendly, browser-based content management product that doesn't require a lot of technical know-how to create, publish and promote engaging content. Built-in tools, including drag-and-drop functionality and a library of templates, help users create one-of-a-kind websites on their own, with plenty of on-board options for improving SEO to enhance visibility and grow their audience. A streamlined dashboard makes it easy to track data and generate reports, and the interface makes it simple to update your site and modify it based on the evolving tastes and needs of your customers. Plus, it offers features to manage workflow and task delegation.

Pros
Percussion is simple to use, with some users going live with their websites within just a few days. Making changes to an existing site is fairly straightforward -- you won't need a big IT department to keep your sites looking great. In addition to its own analytics and reporting capabilities, Percussion integrates with Google Analytics for greater depth and analysis of your content and its performance. Decoupled architecture provides an added level of security and reduces reliance on IT support.

Cons

Despite Percussion's focus on simplicity, not all functions are intuitive and for some, the learning curve can be problematic. The company website notes it updates the product every two months, and depending on the scope of the upgrades, staying up to speed on continual developments may require extra resources.

Rainmaker

rainmakerplatform.com
Expansive tool for stormlike content

Designed by CopyBlogger, Rainmaker transforms typical digital marketing into a turnkey operation. With a focus on growth and enhanced features and capabilities, Rainmaker combines content creation, distribution, and management tools into one resource. Rainmaker ensures all pages are optimized appropriately, and you can access a full suite of audio editing, capture and playback tools.

As a result, Rainmaker makes an excellent resource for those seeking to create a more interactive environment for visitors. Rainmaker also offers a risk-free, 14-day trial to test the platform.

Pros

Users of Rainmaker do not have to worry about installing countless plugins, combing through endless themes or templates, or figuring out how to create and manage complicated codes. The Rainmaker dashboard allows for quick insights into every aspect of your activities, and the system includes CRM tools to keep all relevant information accessible and usable. Since the system is entirely cloud-based, there are no physical hosting requirements, maintenance updates and security system patches to worry about. A Rainmaker subscription automatically includes an SSL certificate and 24/7 customer support.

Start designing your website with one of Rainmaker's themes, or create a custom layout and design to meet your needs. By directly combining all marketing and digital platform requirements and desires into one resource, Rainmaker is able to dramatically reduce your overhead costs. You also have the option of paying for Rainmaker annually or quarterly.

Cons

Rainmaker is currently incapable of hosting APIs or installing other WordPress plugins. Although designed as a marketing platform, the platform does not include internal email or autoresponder features, but it can integrate with AWeber, MailChimp and Infusionsoft.

Salesforce

salesforce.com
Predictive analysis builds leads, drives engagement

As a sales optimization tool, Salesforce really needs no introduction, but its use as a content marketing tool is perhaps less well known. In fact, Salesforce offers a comprehensive content management program called Marketing Cloud that provides a unified location for marketing content across channels, providing a consistent customer experience at every part of the sales funnel. Salesforce Marketing Cloud features an array of tools to make it easy for businesses of all sizes to meet their unique needs, and a dedicated tech team ensures the platform evolves as SEO, SEM and other content-driven processes and algorithms change over time.

Pros

Salesforce uses predictive technology and complex algorithms to automatically track and evaluate customers' preferences in real time so future content can be fully optimized for greater conversions and deeper engagement. Its Journey Builder feature is fully scalable, enabling businesses of all sizes to customize the sales experience at every level based on an in-depth analysis of customer actions. Marketing Cloud also offers an integrative content editor with mobile-optimized templates and drag-and-drop features to facilitate content creation and distribution, as well as single-source distribution so you can launch content across multiple platforms without leaving the interface. Plus, the program allows you to tag content to make it easier to manage and track.

Cons

Although it offers plenty of features, the Salesforce Marketing Cloud user interface can take some getting used to, and it's not always intuitive, creating a learning curve that needs to be taken into account when deciding if it's the right solution for your needs. Part of this issue is due to the frequent upgrades to the Salesforce platform, which may be implemented in different ways over different portions of the platform, detracting from the cohesive experience. Moving between screens or performing some functions can be sluggish, especially in comparison to competing products which, while they may not offer as many features, may "feel" more responsive. Some users have reported issues when using Salesforce on the Chrome OS.

Squarespace

squarespace.com
Square space for hip design

Hip layouts sporting minimalist design are the hallmark of content management tool Squarespace. Squarespace is responsible for the latest layout on NPR.org, evidence that this content management system uses lots of white space and striking graphics to produce a crisp and streamlined look. Established in 2011, this minimalist website creation station offers a website builder, a Web hosting service and a blogging platform.

The content management part of the deal is made easy with portfolios, photo galleries, media players and streamlined text space. Although Squarespace is not free, a price point of less than $10 a month for a basic subscription is a reasonable investment for a high-quality CMS.

Pros
Getting started with Squarespace is a cinch. Sign up and start working on your content management system immediately without downloading or uploading anything. Squarespace went through a huge overhaul of its interface in October 2014, which increased its capacity for content. Access to Getty Images, more than a dozen new templates, cover pages and updates to Android apps all help bring Squarespace to the forefront of the competition.

The software is extreme user-friendly, giving non-techies a treat with easy-to-manage modules and features, such as custom forms and commerce options. Squarespace subscribers even have access to a free logo creator service to help develop their brands. Statistics for Web traffic come standard, and these are located on the same dashboard used for editing. Squarespace handles everything, including automatic upgrades to the system, with full tech support around the clock.

Cons

Choosing Squarespace for your CMS needs means you must use Squarespace for everything — even your Web hosting. This can put a damper on your budget if you already have a Web hosting service, and custom domain names require an annual subscription. Top-of-the-line features are, of course, only available with top-tier subscriptions, and you may need supplements. For any level of detail on your visitor statistics, for instance, you'll need to install Google Analytics, as Squarespace keeps its statistics as minimalist as its sites.

Widen

widen.com
Scalable single-source solution for all your digital assets

Widen's Media Collective is a scalable digital asset management platform designed to let businesses create, gather, edit, collate and distribute all their digital content. A user-friendly interface lets you upload, download, edit and share content from any device, including smartphones and tablets. Built-in features let you control how your content is seen and manipulated within the platform, letting you set permissions based on a wide array of factors and metadata. Additional features let you oversee rights management, set expiration dates for content, track and report activity, and determine how well specific content is performing for greater insight into your campaign.

Pros

Uploading wizards and other intuitive tools make Widen a user-friendly solution for companies with sizable digital assets to manage and distribute. Permissions-based access puts you in control of your digital content to preserve editorial integrity, and a sleek design and cutting-edge technology help ensure fast performance and reliable delivery across all platforms. Additionally, Widen allows across-the-board site branding so you can incorporate your logo, colors and more.

Cons

The current version could benefit from task management features to help keep better track of creation, editing and distribution activities. Like just about any full-featured platform, learning to use all the site's features and determine which ones work best for your needs requires a time investment.

Wix

wix.com
Fast, free, easy website building

If you have been putting off building a website for your business because it seems like a major expense and pain in the neck, Wix. com may be your new best friend. Wix is a fast, free and easy-to-use website building platform that's perfect for beginners, even those who have no clue how to begin. Wix requires absolutely no HTML skills, removing the challenges many face with coding or technology. It also takes care of potential mobility issues, creating a site that works on both desktops and mobile devices. If you are armed with HTML knowledge, you can use your coding skills to increase the functionality and personalization of your content. Wix's powerful website building and hosting platform includes unmatched design capabilities, hundreds of designer-made templates, eCommerce functionality, an app market, email marketing solutions and a variety of tailored online products for specific business verticals.

Pros

Easy, easy, easy is the biggest benefit of Wix. You're granted access to hundreds of template designs that you can customize with the features you want for a personalized appearance. Publishing your content is also a breeze. Wix uses a drag-and-drop drop method that lets you place content where you want it; you can then resize and modify it right on the screen. Built-in tools let you quickly edit content and images while one-click mobile optimization gives mobile devices access without glitchy layouts or lag times. Google Analytics is included with all basic Wix sites, allowing you to monitor what your site visitors are doing and what they're looking for.

Cons

Although you can get access to website templates and hosting for free, the no-cost plan doesn't really supply a business with everything it needs. For starters, you'll be stuck with wix.com in your site address unless you upgrade to a paid subscription. Moving to the lowest-priced plan gives you 500 MB of storage and 1GB of bandwidth. While this is not a bad starting point for most sites, your lowest-level site will be peppered with Wix-branded ads, and you'll lack access to any of the premium apps. You'll also have to pay separately for a domain name, a perk that's included with higher-priced plans.

It always pays to double-check the introductory prices offered by any hosting provider. Introductory prices tend to increase after the first year of service, and you may be saddled with a much higher annual fee when you renew.

WordPress

wordpress.com
Simple-to-use, go-to standard with plenty of bells and whistles

WordPress is a leader in website and blog creation and management, offering both free and hosted versions that are used by millions of websites. Although it may have initially gained its fame as a free site for blogs and simple websites, today the platform offers a full suite of website design tools and powerful hosting to make it easy for businesses of all sizes to build great-looking and high-performing websites. Hundreds of plugins make it easy to share on social networks, and analytic tools and reporting provide a detailed view of performance to serve as the basis for future marketing efforts.

Pros

Thanks in part to its history as a free site and blog provider, the user interface has had a lot of revisions and tweaks over the years, resulting in a dashboard that's very user-friendly. In addition to its web support team, a community of highly engaged users – including many experienced designers – is always at the ready to provide troubleshooting guidance as well as design and optimization tips.

There are hundreds of templates to get your site up and running, and loads of plugin tools (including e-commerce options) to make it as customized as you like. With its roots in blogging and content creation, WordPress makes it incredibly easy to create and distribute marketing content that's optimized for SEO, and responsive themes also make creating mobile-friendly sites a relatively easy task.

Cons

Although it offers some beautiful design templates, customizing those templates takes some coding know-how and a fair degree of patience. Certain features like blogging are well-established and intuitive, but others have a bit of a learning curve before users can take advantage of all they can offer. Lots of developers releasing lots of plugins can make quality control a little spotty. Making changes to your site requires a few clicks to publish the site in order to see the end result, and because there are so many plugins and options, getting up to speed initially and determining which options you want and need can take some time.

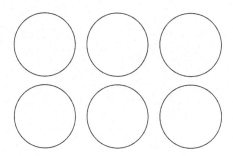

Content Marketing Conference Speakers

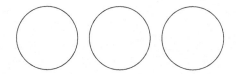

Speaker Podcasts

Hear the stories behind these fabulous tools by listening to interviews with the founders and CEOs. Visit *http://www.contentmarketingconference.com/podcasts/* to tune in.

Hana Abaza
VP of Marketing
UberFlip
@HanaAbaza

Hana Abaza is the VP Marketing at Uberflip, a content platform that helps marketers create, manage and optimize content experiences at every stage of the funnel. She combines a data-driven approach with her knack for communicating inspired tech solution to mainstream audiences to get results. Hana is also a dynamic speaker and contributor to Forbes, Entrepreneur.com, CMO.com and other industry publications. Find her on twitter @HanaAbaza

Jessica Ann
CEO and Creative Director
Jessica Ann Media
@itsjessicann

Jessica Ann is the CEO and Creative Director of Jessica Ann Media {JAM}, a creative agency that develops compelling content for top-tier brands. With a Master's Degree in Communications from Johns Hopkins University, Jessica inspires advocates for Fortune 500 companies through shared emotions and experiences, driving hundreds of thousands of dollars in revenue in a way that's authentic and fun. Jessica is an experienced news producer for national media outlets such as NBC Newschannel and XM Radio in Washington, D.C. Her work has been featured in The Huffington Post, Elephant Journal, and The Good Men Project. She was an official speaker at SXSW Interactive in March of 2016.

Tim Ash

CEO & Founder
Site Tuners
@tim_ash

Tim is a highly-regarded presenter and keynote speaker at SES, eMetrics, PPC Summit, Affiliate Summit, PubCon, SMX, OMS, AffCon, LeadsCon, Internet Retailer, and eComXpo. He is the founder and chairperson of ConversionConference.com the first international conference series focused on improving online conversions. Tim is a contributing columnist to several publications including ClickZ, Website Magazine, DM News, Visibility Magazine, Search Marketing Standard, Search Engine Marketing Journal, and Electronic Retailer Online Strategies magazine. He is the host of the weekly Landing Page Optimization show and podcast on WebmasterRadio.fm. Over the past 15 years, Tim has helped a number of major US and international brands to develop successful web-based initiatives. Companies like Google, Expedia, Kodak, eHarmony, Facebook, American Express, Canon, Nestle, Symantec, Intuit, AutoDesk and many others have benefitted from Tim's deep understanding and innovative perspective. Since 1995, he has authored more than 100 published articles. In addition, Tim is the online voice of conversion optimization as the host of the Landing Page Optimization podcast on WebmasterRadio.fm.

Josh Bernoff

Author, Writing Without Bullshit Author,
Groundswell, Chief Trouble Maker
WithoutBullshit.com
@jbernoff

Josh has been a professional writer since 1982. He coauthored three books on business strategy, including Groundswell, which was a bestseller. He's passionate about clear, brief, fascinating communication. HarperBusiness will publish his new book, Writing Without Bullshit, in September 2016. Josh blogs every weekday about writing, communication, and bullshit. His blog generated over 1 million views in its first year. For 20 years at Forrester Research, he wrote and edited reports on the future of technology. As Senior Vice President, Idea Development, he identified, developed, and promoted Forrester's most powerful and influential ideas. Josh is also the CEO of wellnesscampaign.org, a non-profit organization dedicated to the pursuit of wellness through changing habits.

Christopher Bowler

Senior Vice President, Social Media and Content Marketing
Razorfish
@chrisrbowler

Chris believes "Social Media" and "Content Marketing" don't have to be complicated. Simply put, it's really just about being you. And that counts for a brand or a business too. But the key is to offer something of value which others will respond to and share. His role at Razorfish is to lead clients forward in the use of ever-evolving social media and content marketing channels. Eighty-five percent of the time, this is acting as a cheerleader/evangelist/therapist/trailblazer to drive idea development and test-and-learn programs. This all started with online services like AOL and Prodigy, where Chris launched the first online ad campaigns for clients, and later, on the burgeoning Internet, introduced the first new product launch for a major appliance company. He started in offline advertising with Campbell Mithun in Minneapolis, before jumping into the digital pool at Agency.com, where he led the digital media and search engine marketing practice. He's spoken at industry conferences such as SXSW, ad:tech, Content Marketing Conference and WOMMA.

Bill Carmody

CEO
Trepoint
@BillCarmody

Bill is the founder and CEO of Trepoint, a proud international speaker, and @Inc columnist. He's an inspirational leader who enjoys solving problems and creating breakthroughs in himself and others. As a 22-year digital marketing change agent, he empowers and supports people brave enough to build a better future. An entrepreneur since the age of 12, Bill knows what it takes to move great ideas into successful marketing programs. In 2008, Bill launched Trepoint In 2008, a digital marketing boutique agency, to help mid-market "Challenger Brands" become leaders in their space, especially those in CPG, B2B Technology, and Entertainment. Over the years he has worked with a companies to improve the impact of their marketing including Miller Genuine Draft, Trinchero Family Estates (Sutter Home and Menage a Trois), Windsor Foods (Jose Ole, Tai Pei, and Ling Ling), Dunkin' Donuts, EMC and RSA.

Will Dailey
@willdailey

Will Dailey is an independent American recording artist, performer and producer. His sound has been described as having a rich vintage vibe while having a firm appreciation of AM rock, pop and big hooks. Based out of Boston, he is a five-time winner of the Boston Music Awards: Best Male Singer-Songwriter 2006, 2009 and 2012 and Album of the Year and Artist of the Year 2014.

Melanie Deziel
Director of Creative Strategy
MDeziel Media
@mdeziel

As Creative Strategist at Time Inc., Melanie creates innovative branded content campaigns that span 25+ print and digital properties, including Sports Illustrated, People, Fortune, Entertainment Weekly, Health and Travel+Leisure. She has done content strategy and social strategy for both HuffPost Partner Studio and The New York Times's T Brand Studio, where she created the OMMA Award winning "Women Inmates" piece for Netflix's Orange Is The New Black.

Andrea Fryrear

Content Marketer & Agile Marketing Evangelist, SurveyGizmo
Author, Agile Marketing Styles
@AndreaFryrear

Andrea is confessed content marketing nerd, fervent agile marketing evangelist, and a Certified Scrum Master and Certified Scrum Product Owner. She's a firm believer in Agile's potential to help support her fellow content marketers with the long-term production of stellar content. You can find her detailed coverage of all things content and agile over at MarketerGizmo.com, which she edits and manages. Andrea is also the author of the eBook Agile Marketing Styles: Your Guide to Finding the Right Agile Approach For Your Marketing Team.

Kindra Hall

@kindramhall

Kindra is an award-winning columnist, author, and national champion storyteller. As a former Director of Marketing and VP of Sales, Kindra discovered the most effective method for capturing attention and increasing revenue—great storytelling. Kindra's work has been featured in SUCCESS Magazine and behind the scenes in New York Times best selling books. A former board member of the National Storytelling Network, and with a Master's Degree in Org Comm & Management, Kindra now teaches innovative brands and executives to close more sales, become better leaders and blow up brands with the irresistible power of strategic storytelling.

Nancy Harhut

Chief Creative Officer
Wilde Agency
@nharhut

A frequent speaker at industry conferences, Nancy's shared her passion with audiences from Moscow (as the only American on the speaker's roster) to the U.S. Department of Defense (twice). Along the way, she's been named NEDMA Direct Marketer of the Year, Ad Club Top 100 Creative Influencer, OMI Top 40 Digital Marketing Strategist, and Andi Emerson Award recipient. Prior to Wilde Agency, Nancy held senior creative management positions with Hill Holliday, Mullen and Digitas. She and her teams have won over 150 awards for digital and direct marketing effectiveness.

Anum Hussain

Senior Growth Marketer
HubSpot
@anum

As a Senior Growth Marketer at HubSpot, Anum leads content strategy and demand generation for HubSpot's sales products while managing an incredible squad of growth marketers who spend every day researching, executing, and experimenting with content – spanning everything from offers to emails to nurturing. Outside of HubSpot, Anum continues geeking out over marketing: She co-authored Twitter for Dummies, was recently named BetaBoston's 25 Under 25, and has been rated a top 5 INBOUND speaker two years in a row. When she's not marketing, Anum enjoys spending time with her family, eating cookie cakes, and talking about Harry Potter. In fact, Beyonce is her patronus.

Greg Jarboe

President and Co-founder
SEO-PR
@gregjarboe

Greg Jarboe is the President and co-founder of SEO-PR, a content marketing agency. He is also the author of YouTube and Video Marketing: An Hour a Day as well as a contributor to Strategic Digital Marketing: Top Digital Experts Share the Formula for Tangible Returns on Your Marketing Investment, Complete B2B Online Marketing, and Enchantment: The Art of Changing Hearts, Minds, and Actions. He is also profiled in Online Marketing Heroes: Interviews with 25 Successful Online Marketing Gurus. He's on the faculty at the Rutgers Business School and Market Motive. He writes for ClickZ and ReelSEO. He is also a frequent speaker at industry conferences.

Jeff Julian

Chief Marketing Officer, AJi
Author, Agile Marketing: Building Endurance for your Content Marketing Teams

Jeff Julian is the Chief Marketing Officer for AJi, a digital agency based in Kansas City. Jeff has been helping companies, such as Microsoft, develop content strategies for over ten years after he launched one of the largest blogging communities, Geekswithblogs.net. He has been a web developer since 1994, a best-selling author of a book on content management system development, and a Microsoft Most Valuable Professional in XML and SharePoint. Jeff has recently finished a book titled, Agile Marketing: Building Endurance for your Content Marketing Teams.

Larry Kim

Founder
WordStream
@larrykim

Larry Kim is the founder of WordStream, a PPC management software and services company whose free PPC and keyword research tools have been used by more than a million internet marketers worldwide. Larry has been named the most influential PPC marketer in the world for the last two years by PPC Hero and 3QDigital, and his internet marketing blog is read by nearly a million visitors every month. Larry is a columnist for Search Engine Land, Search Engine Watch, Hubspot, Moz, Inc Magazine, Marketing Profs, and dozens of other publications.

Kathy Klotz-Guest, MA, MBA

Storyteller, Creative Facilitator, Speaker and Improviser
KeepingItHuman
@kathyklotzguest

Kathy Klotz-Guest, MA, MBA, is a business storyteller and speaker. Founder of Keeping it Human, she helps organizations turn jargon-monoxide into compelling stories that move people to action. It's her mission to turn teams into powerful storytellers. Kathy is also a comic improviser and writer who performs regularly. She is the author of two books on humor, content, and storytelling (The Executive's Bedtime Guide series) and is the co-author of an upcoming book on the future of business storytelling (2016). Her work has been published in Convince and Convert, Marketing Profs, and Customer Think among other publications. Her favorite audience is still her seven-year-old son.

Bryan Kramer

Author, Shareology & Human to Human
CEO, PureMatter
@bryankramer

Bryan Kramer is a bestselling author, TED speaker and CEO who consults Fortune 500 clients such as IBM, Cisco and Pitney Bowes on humanizing business. He is one of the world's foremost leaders in the art and science of sharing, and has been credited with shaping the #H2H human business movement in marketing and social. He's also a global keynote speaker, bestselling author and strategist who consults Fortune 500 clients such as IBM, Cisco and Pitney Bowes on humanizing business through social media. Bryan has been named a "Top 25 Social Influencer to Follow" by Forbes, one of the "100 Most Influential Tech People On Twitter" by Business Insider, and one of the "Top 50 Social CEOs on Twitter Globally" by The Huffington Post. Bryan's latest book, Shareology, made the USA Today's Top 150 Book List the week of its release, as well as #1 on Amazon in four categories including Business & Planning.

Arnie Kuenn

CEO
Vertical Measures
@ArnieK

Arnie Kuenn is the CEO of Vertical Measures, a full-service Internet marketing agency dedicated to helping clients drive profitable growth through SEO & content marketing. Arnie has held executive positions in the world of new technologies and marketing for more than 25 years. Mr. Kuenn is a founder of the Arizona Interactive Marketing Association (AZIMA). Arnie speaks at events around the world and has personally trained more than 3,000 students on content marketing. He recently published his second book, Content Marketing Works, with his son Brad.

Erica McGillivray

Senior Community Manager
Moz
@emcgillivray

Erica McGillivray is a die-hard geek who spends a ridiculous amount of time being nerdy, both professionally and personally. At Moz, she's the senior community manager and wrangles a community of over 500,000 members, co-runs the annual MozCon, and works on whatever else is thrown her way. She's also a founder of GeekGirlCon, a nonprofit run by volunteers that celebrates and supports geeky women with events and conventions. In her spare time, Erica's a published author and has a comic book collection that's an earthquake hazard.

David McInnis

Founder, CEO
Cranberry
@giantcranberry

David McInnis is the founder of PRWeb, the first online content marketing platform for press releases. A lifetime entrepreneur with ventures that range from Internet technology to candy manufacturing and 3D rapid manufacturing, David has developed an affinity with smaller businesses and startups, helping them to tell their stories and get noticed. His latest venture, Cranberry, is a content amplification platform that emphasizes the importance of deep customer relationships through content. Cranberry recently acquired WebmasterRadio.fm and is relaunching the service under CranberryRadio.fm.

Chad Pollitt

VP of Audience and Co-Founder
Relevance

Chad Pollitt is one of the top five content marketing thought leaders and top 20 CMO influencers recognized by Nice and Onalytica. He is currently the VP of Audience and Co-Founder of Relevance, a digital magazine, agency and events company focused on content research, strategy, promotion and marketing. His books, The Content Promotion Manifesto and 51 Things Your Mother Taught You About Inbound Marketing, helped his company earn a spot on a Forbes Top 100 list. He's a decorated Veteran of Operation Iraqi Freedom and former Army Commander, and currently an Adjunct Professor of Internet Marketing at the Indiana University Kelley School of Business. Tune in to Chad and tap into his fourteen years of success with brands of all sizes, accelerating revenue with innovative methods and tactics along the way.

Mike Roberts

Founder and CEO
SpyFu, Inc.
@mrspy

SpyFu President and Founder Mike Roberts understands search marketing from different angles. Having founded SpyFu in 2006 and introduced Recon Files in 2010, he led the charge in transforming the way search marketers craft their strategies in PPC and SEO. His creations fuel success for many entrepreneurs, but as SpyFu President, Mike puts himself in the mind of a search marketer just trying to make sense of challenges ahead.

Neal Schaffer

President
Maximize Your Social
@NealSchaffer

Neal Schaffer is a recognized innovative leader in the world of business social media. In addition to being named one of marketing's ten biggest thought leaders by CMO.com, Neal has also been recognized as a Forbes Top 50 Social Media Power Influencer two years in a row as well as a Forbes Top 5 Social Sales Influencer. A global social media keynote speaker who has appeared on 4 continents at more than 200 events since 2009, Neal is the author of three social media books, including the definitive book on social media strategy Maximize Your Social. In addition to speaking and consulting, Neal also teaches social media marketing at Rutgers University and the Irish Management Institute and is the founder of the Social Media Center of Excellence, a community dedicated to propagating best practices amongst social media marketing professionals.

Sudhir Sharma

Director, Acquisition Marketing
Movoto
@sudhirpsharma

Sudhir is Director, Acquisition Marketing at Movoto.com where he leads a team of traffic acquisition & web analytics experts. He is responsible for generating target audience traffic by leveraging "non paid media" strategies and tactics and by building synergies between Paid, Social, Content, PR, and user community. Prior to Movoto, Sudhir worked with BrightEdge, Adobe and EfficientFrontier in different roles responsible for lead generation, analytics and positioning the companies in their space. Sudhir is passionate about learning & execution of Customer Acquisition, Growth Hacking, Web Analytics, Conversion Rate Optimization and Lean & Scrappy Marketing. He is a Google Analytics certified professional, and holds a master's in computer science from California State University, Chico. In his free time, Sudhir skis and likes to play volleyball.

Josh Steimle

CEO
MWI
@joshsteimle

Josh Steimle is an author, speaker, and entrepreneur. He has written over 200 articles for publications like Forbes, Mashable, TechCrunch, and Time, and is the author of Chief Marketing Officers at Work: How Top Marketers Build Customer Loyalty. Steimle is a TEDx speaker and has presented at conferences like ClickZ Live, Adtech, Social Media Week. He is also the founder and CEO of MWI, a digital marketing firm he founded in 1999 with offices in Hong Kong and the U.S. Steimle was recently recognized by Entrepreneur magazine as one of 50 Online Marketing Influencers To Watch in 2016.

Mathew Sweezey

Principal of Marketing Insights
Salesforce.com
@msweezey

Mathew is Principal of Marketing Insights for Salesforce.com, and regarded as one of the top minds on the future of Marketing. A consummate researcher, writer, and thinker, Mathew's is the author of Marketing Automation for Dummies, and working on his next book now. His research is often cited leading publications such as Mashable, VentureBeat, CMO.com, Forbes, and numerous others. Mathew also frequently speaks at conferences around the world including Content Marketing World, Dreamforce, Argyle CMO Summit, Connections, IMW, DX3.

Ryan Urban

CEO and Co-Founder
Bounce Exchange
@BounceExchange

Ryan Urban is the CoFounder and CEO of Bounce Exchange, Inc. The company provides a machine learning platform that is employed by marketers to automate conversion rate optimization and user acquisition. Ryan was formerly Director of Acquisition at Bonobos and prior to that, Brickhouse Security. He has served on the advisory boards of both BabyAge.com and Bonobos. He holds an MBA from Fairleigh Dickinson University.

Amit Vyas

CEO
Nexa – Dubai
@Dubai_CEOs

Amit Vyas is one of the co-founding members of WVSS and continues to be the company's strategic driving force. A genuine tech-entrepreneur and online marketing expert, Amit is successfully guiding the company's growth through technology investments, acquisitions, new product lines and strategic partnerships. Prior to the founding of the starting company WVSS, Amit was based in the UK, owning and managing various businesses that boasted major international clients. Amit holds a BSC (Hons) degree in Computer Science and Business Management from Aston University in the UK. Amit is also currently the Executive President of Blogymate.com – a social blogging platform with over 500,000 members and the Co-Founder and Partner of iKnowledgy – a innovative customer feedback platform that boasts a blue-chip client list.

Byron White

Chair, Content Marketing Conference
CEO, WriterAccess
@byronwhite

Byron White is a content marketing revolutionary, serial entrepreneur, published author, popular speaker, and great storyteller. He is the founder and CEO of WriterAccess, a cloud-based platform that offers access to writers, editors, translators and content strategists who deliver content to customers ranging from SMBs to agencies to Fortune 500s. He is also the founder and chair of Content Marketing Conference, an annual gathering of companies, writers, industry experts and thought leaders.

Jon Wuebben

CEO
Content Launch
@jonwuebben

Jon Wuebben is the CEO of Content Launch, which offers the first content marketing software built for small and medium sized businesses (SMB's) and small agencies. Content Launch also provides content writing and content strategy services for hundreds of companies and digital agencies. His book, "Content is Currency: Developing Powerful Content for Web & Mobile," helps businesses learn how to plan, create, distribute and manage content. "Content is Currency" has been published in six countries worldwide. Jon has spoken at Content Marketing World, Online Marketing Summit, South by Southwest (SXSW) and for many organizations and industry groups in the areas of content marketing, mobile marketing and entrepreneurship. He has been listed as a thought leader in the content marketing space by countless publications since 2008. Jon has an MBA in International Marketing from Thunderbird, The American Graduate School of International Management. He is also the author of "Content Rich: Writing Your Way to Wealth on the Web". In the political world, he has worked for Senator John McCain, Vice President Dan Quayle and the Republican National Convention.

Dennis Yu

CEO and Founder
BlitzMetrics
@dennisyu

Dennis Yu is CEO of BlitzMetrics, a Facebook analytics and optimization software company. Before founding BlitzMetrics, he was an executive at Yahoo!, managing analytics and paid search. Dennis has been interviewed by National Public Radio, KTLA-TV and other media outlets, as has counseled the Federal Trade Commission on privacy issues for social networks. He has spoken at the Search Marketing Expo, HostingCon, Search Engine Strategies, Web 2.0, The American Marketing Association, Conversational Commerce Conference, UltraLight Startups, MIVA Merchant PPC Summit, PubCon, Online Marketing Conference, and other national and international conferences.

CPSIA information can be obtained at www.ICGtesting.com
Printed in the USA
BVOW06s1737110516

447603BV00004B/5/P